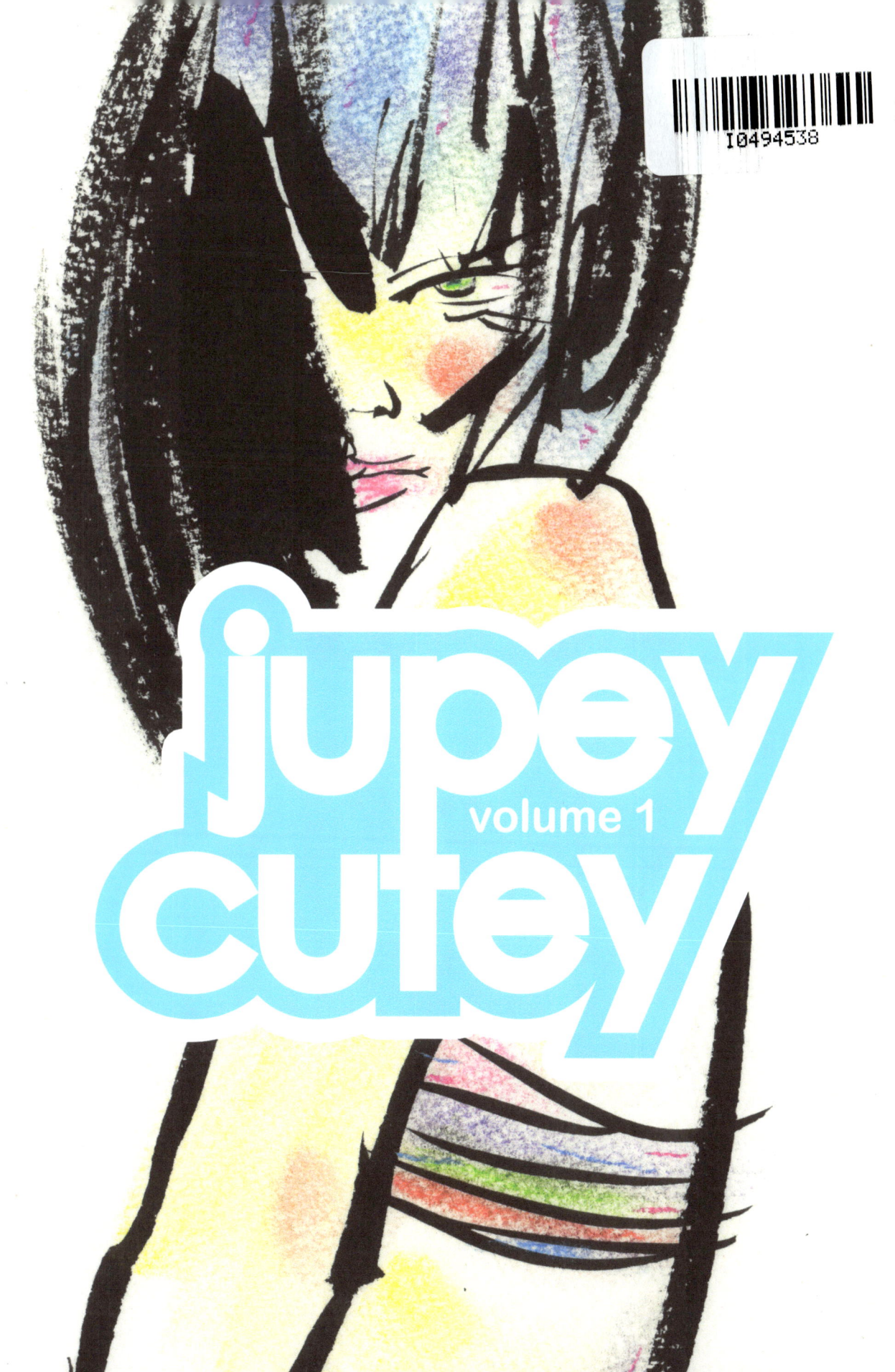

jupey
cutey
volume 1

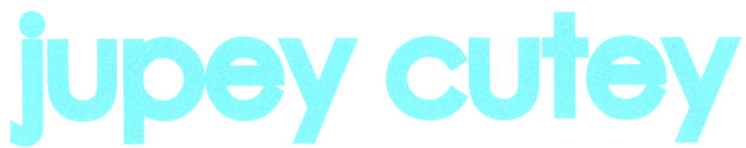

volume 1
works from 2010-2013

Published by jupey krusho
4821 Lankershim Blvd F243
North Hollywood, CA 91601

Printed in the USA
Distributed worldwide by jupey krusho

For information about special sales and premium purchase
please contact jupey at info@jupeykrusho.com.

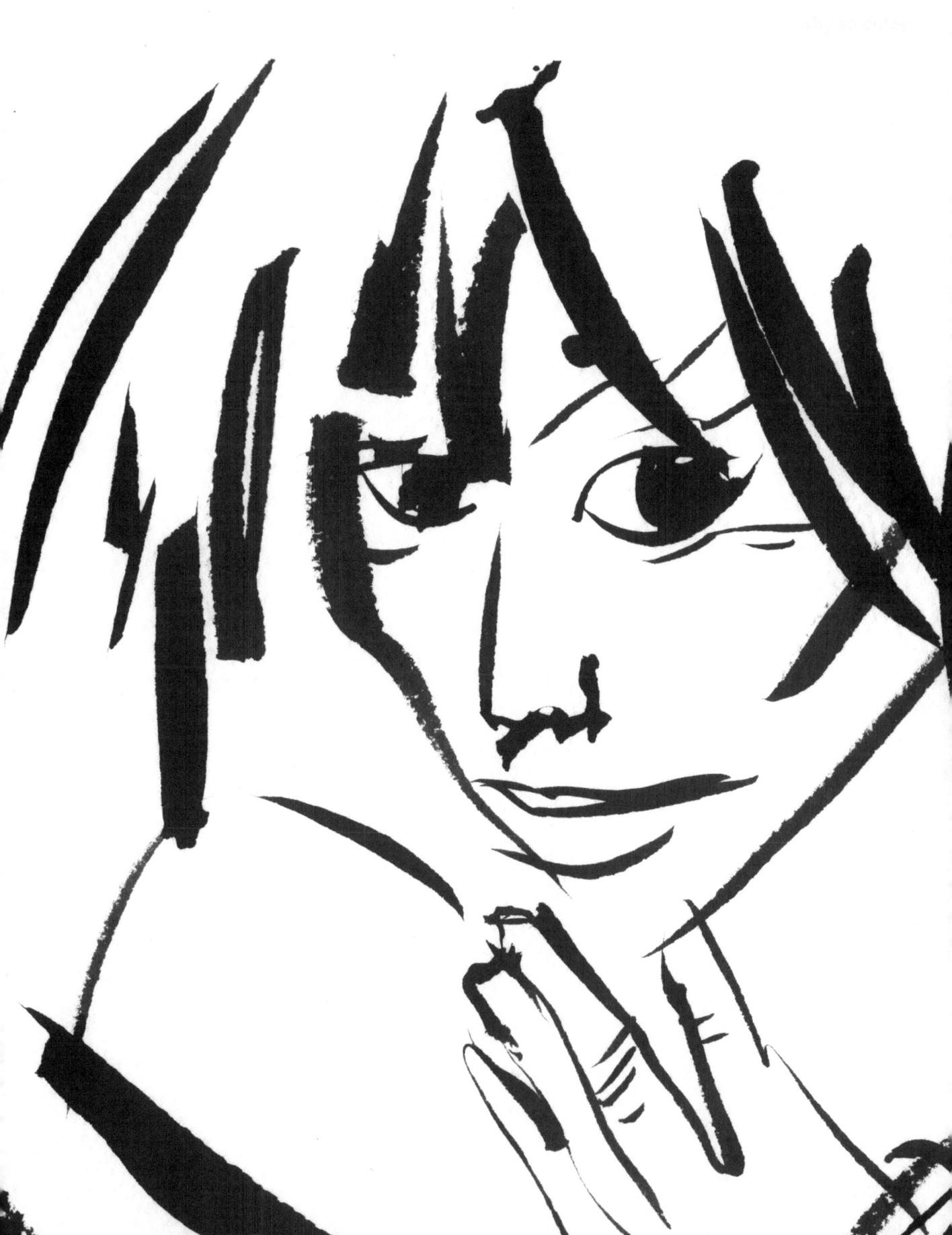

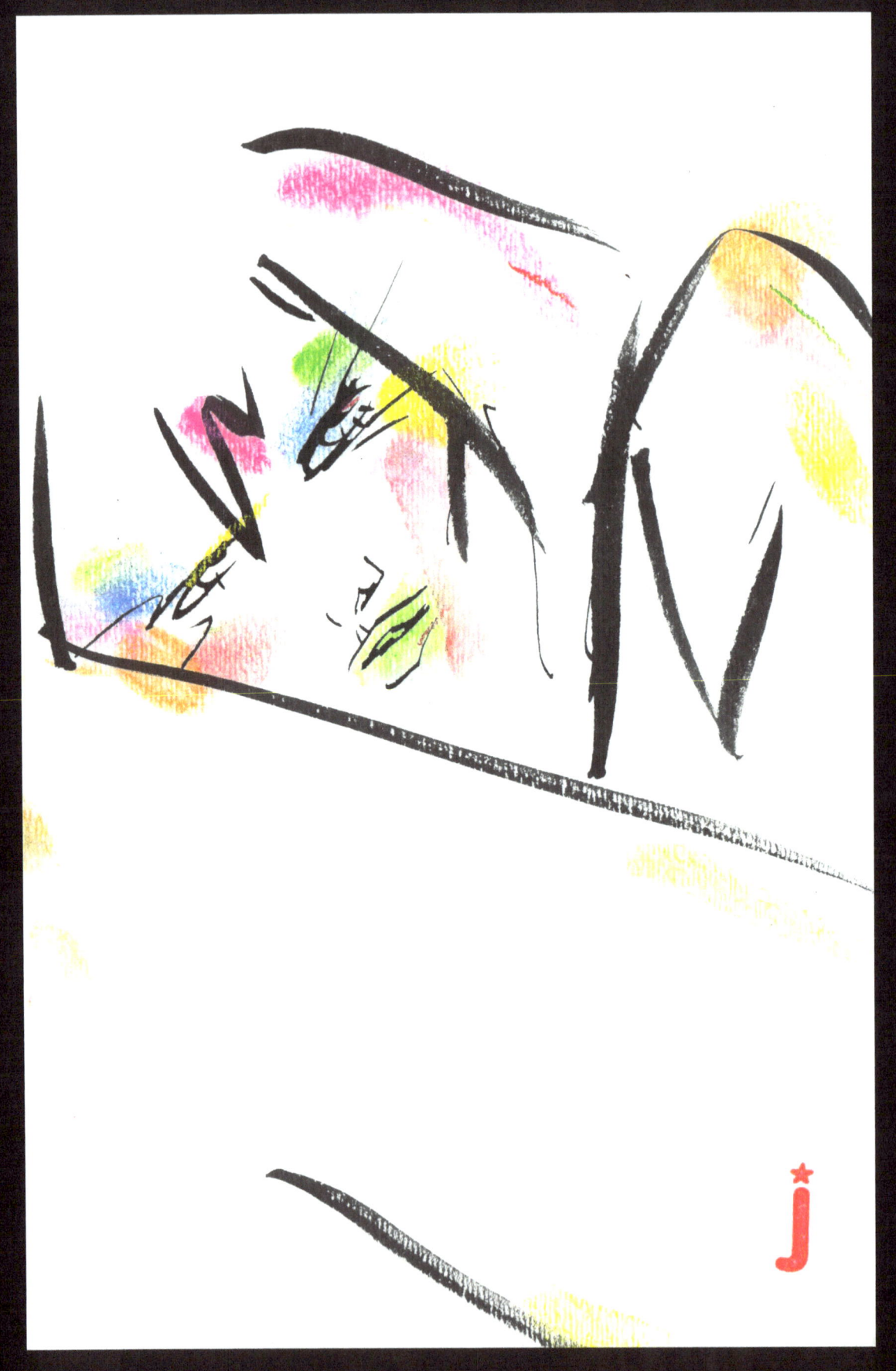

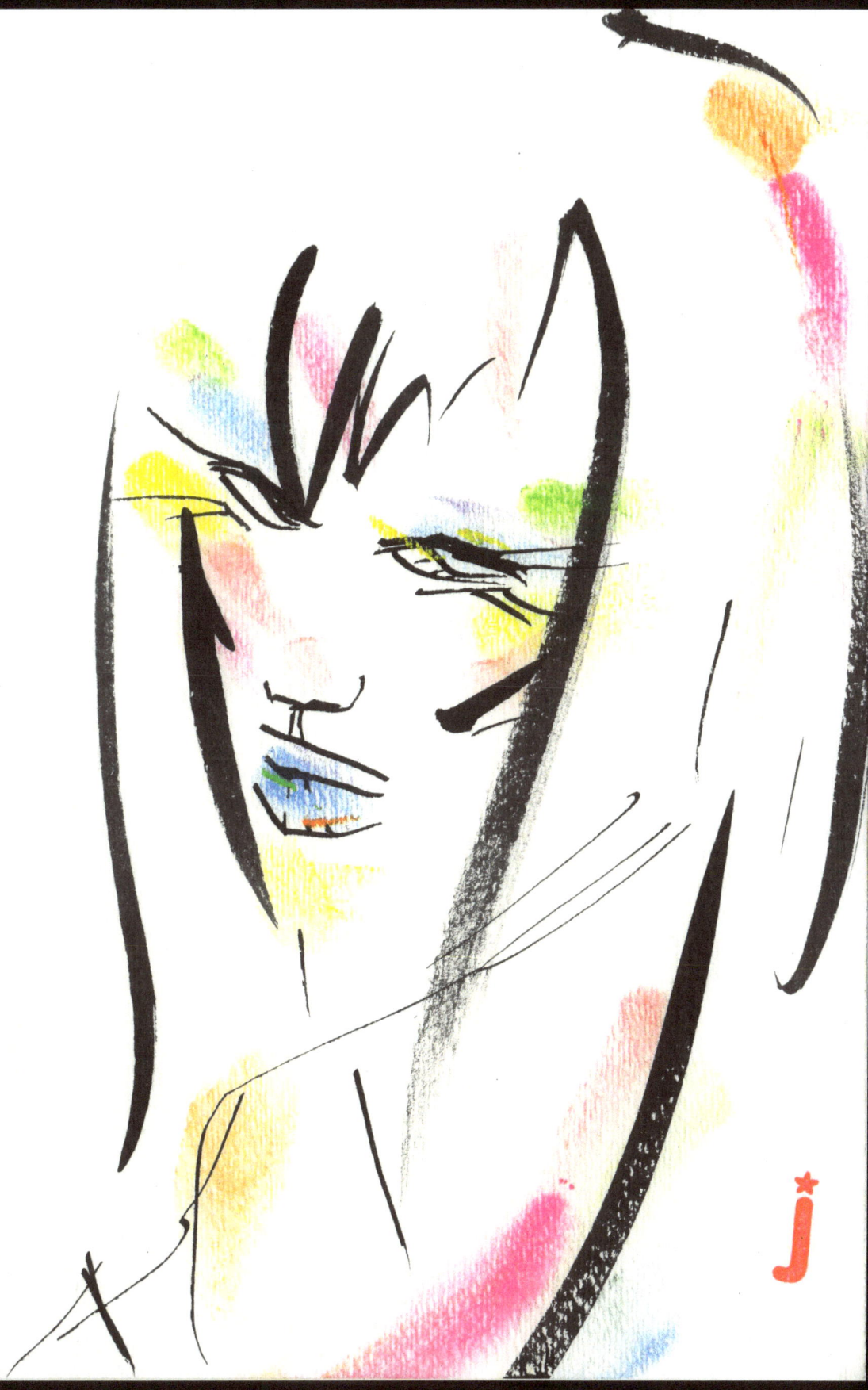

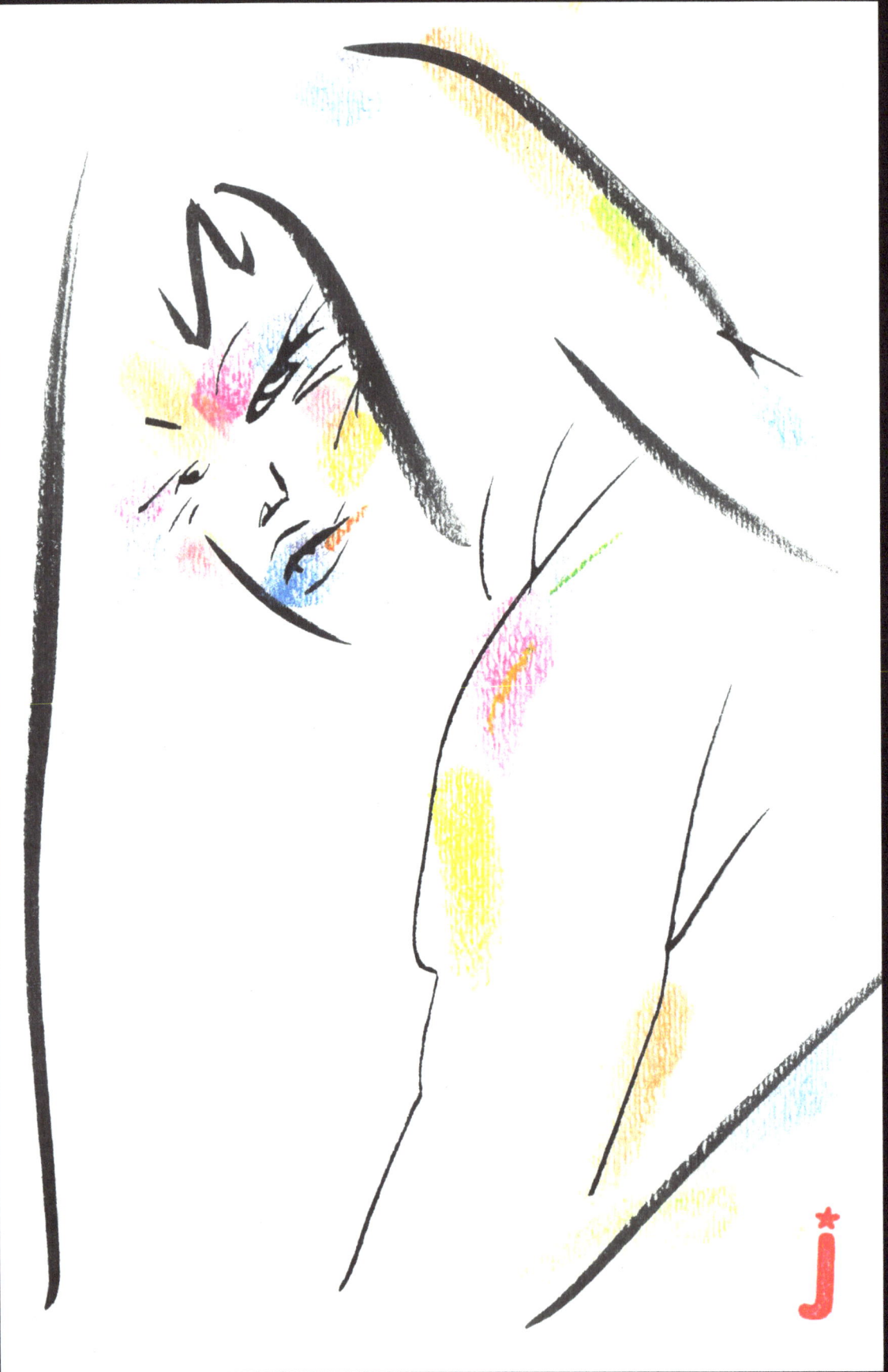

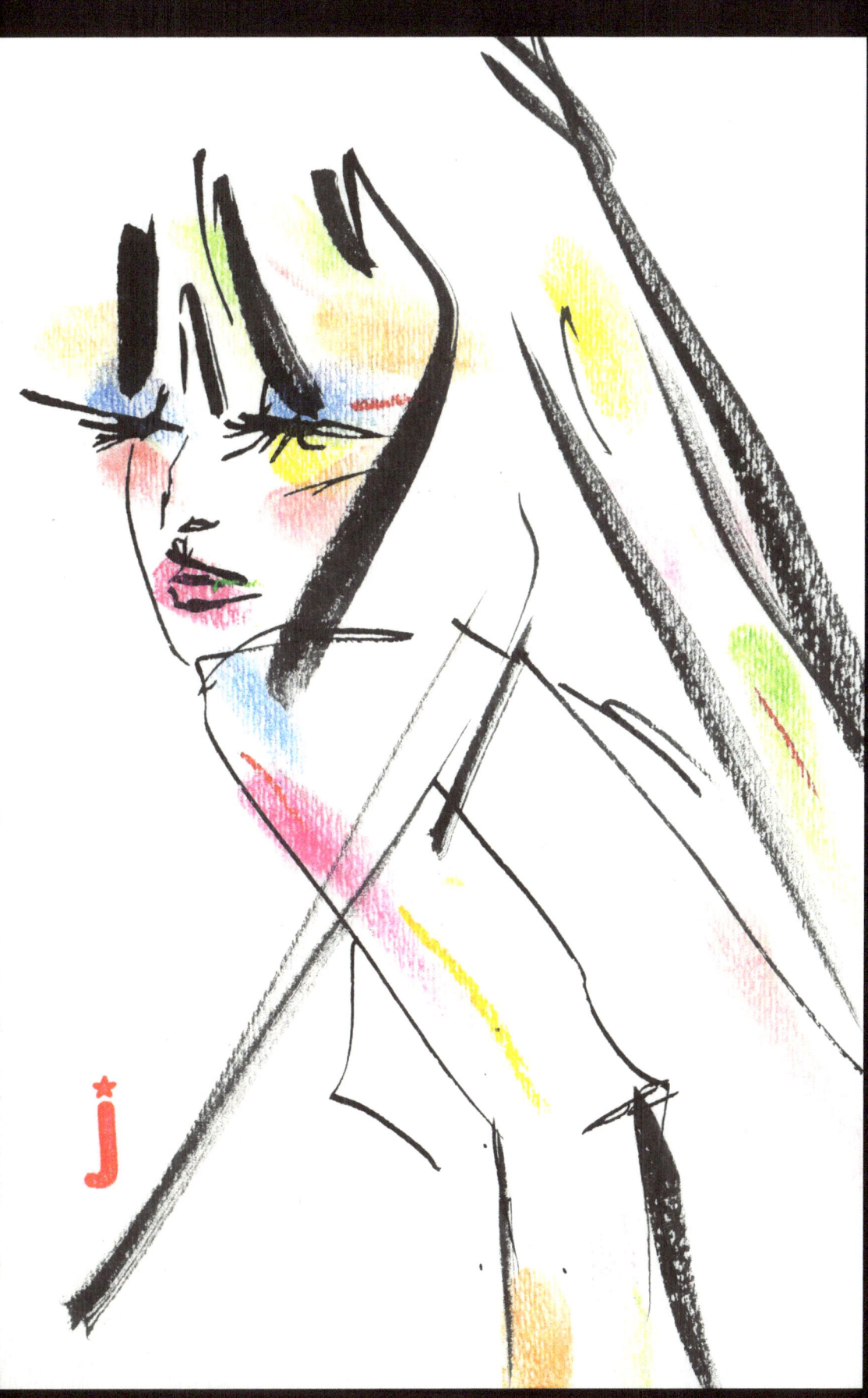

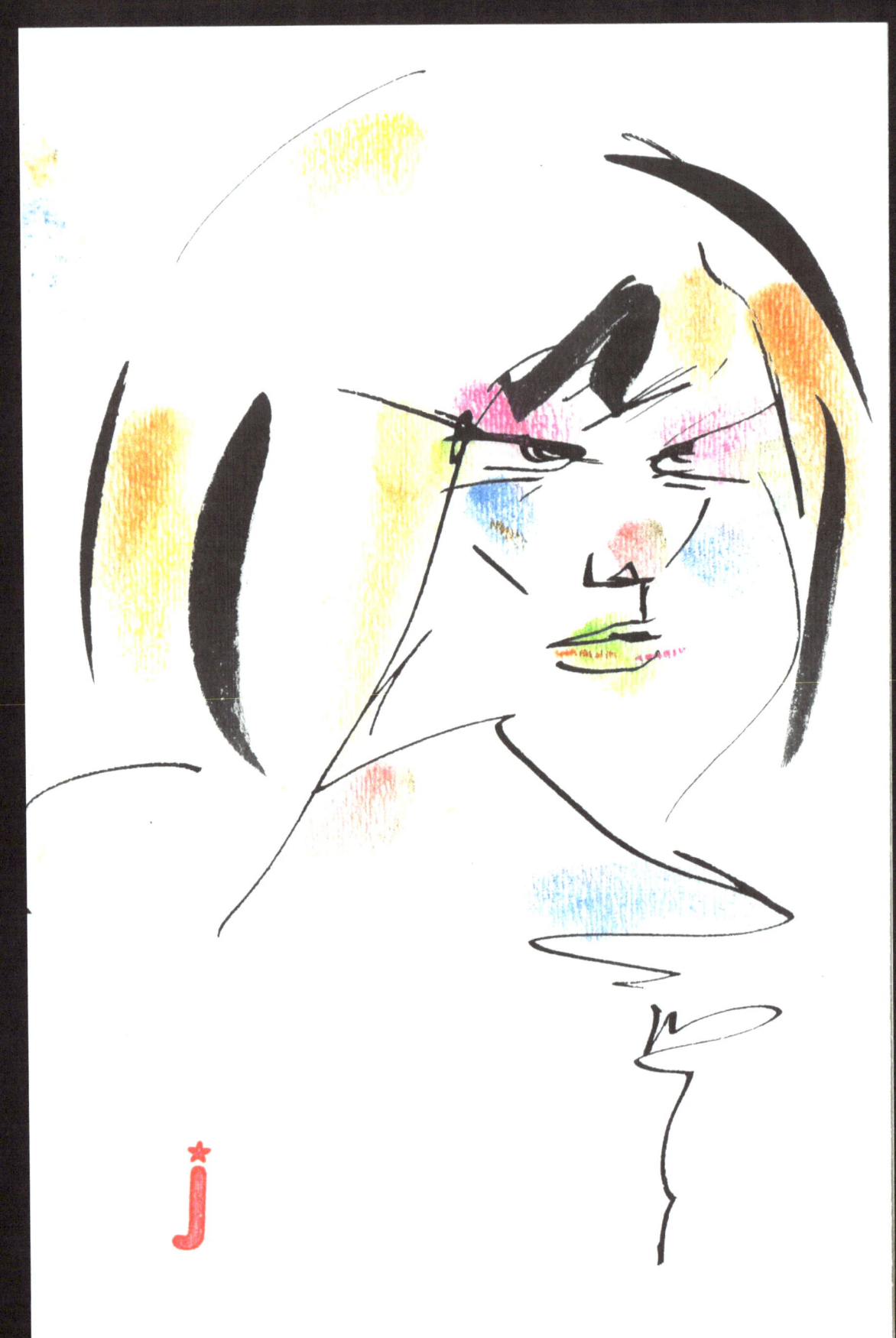

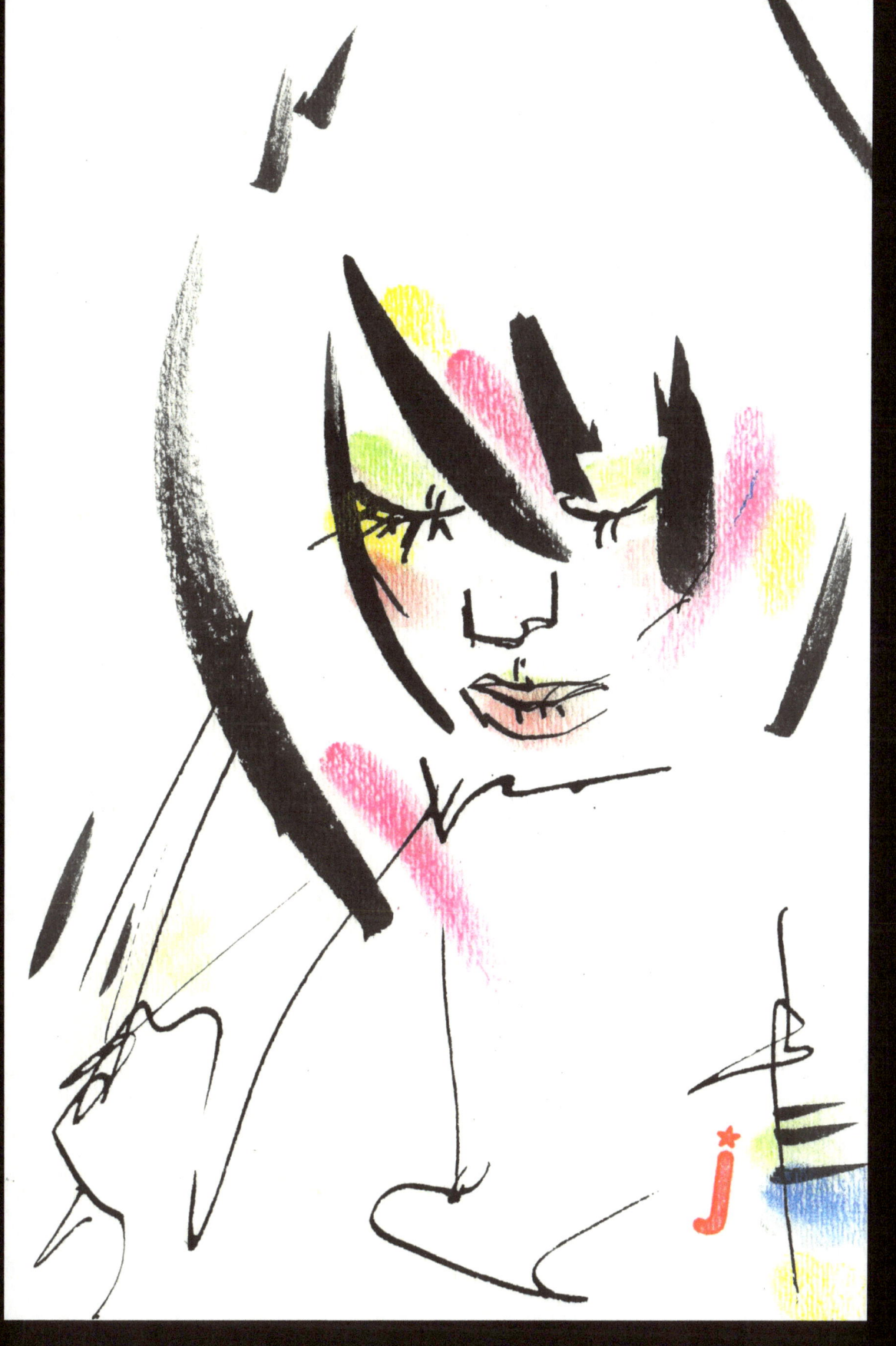

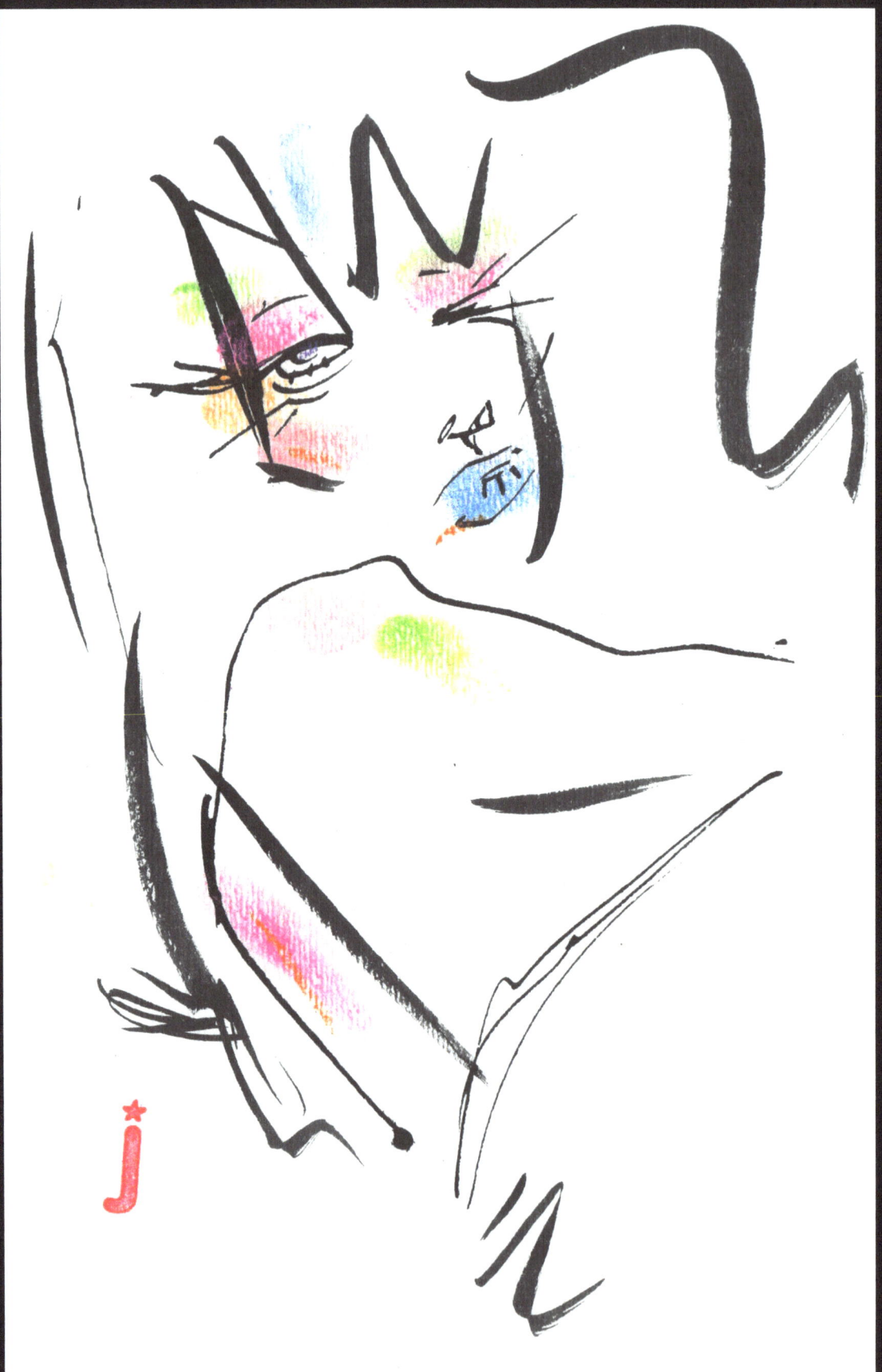

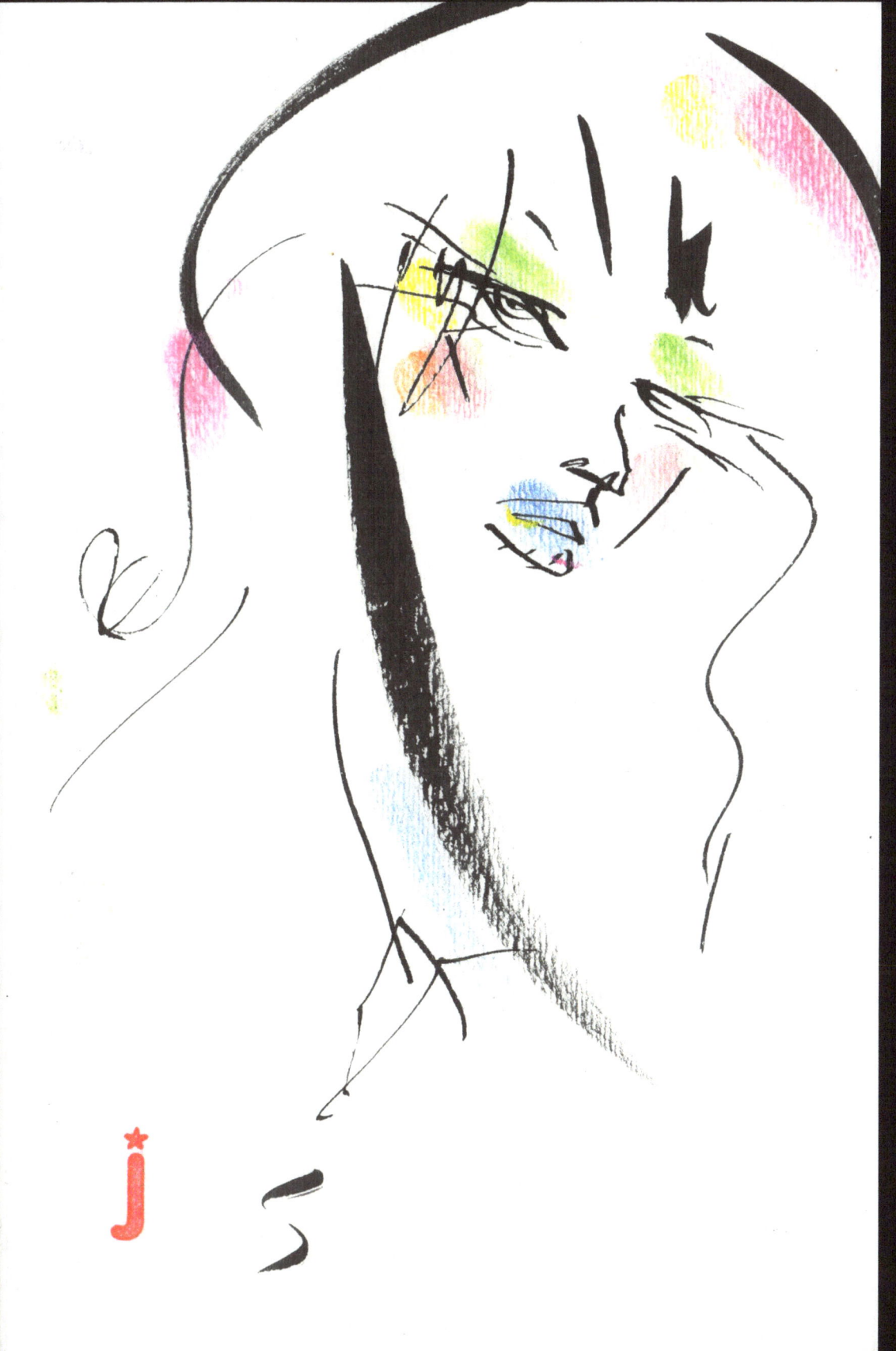

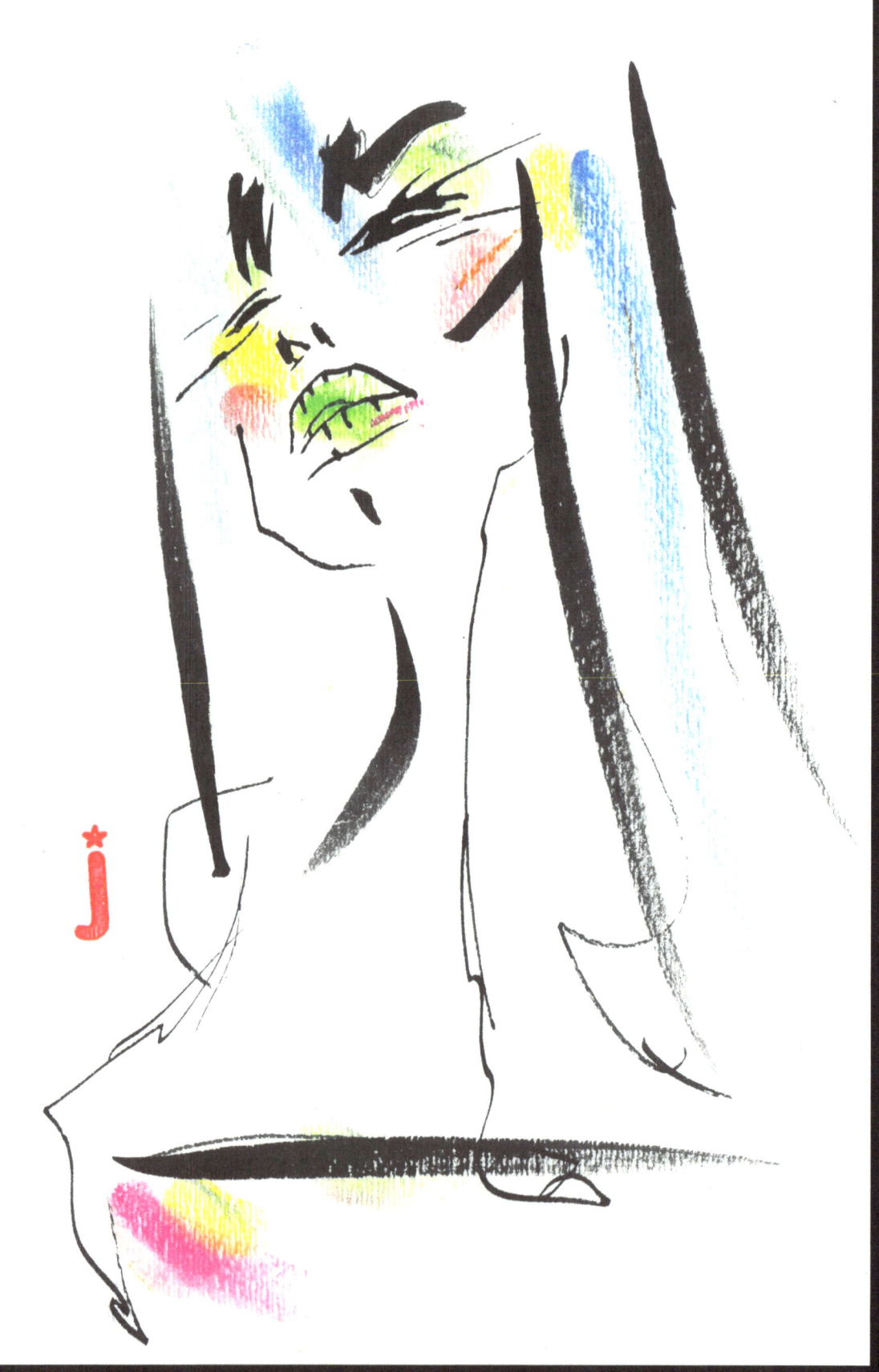

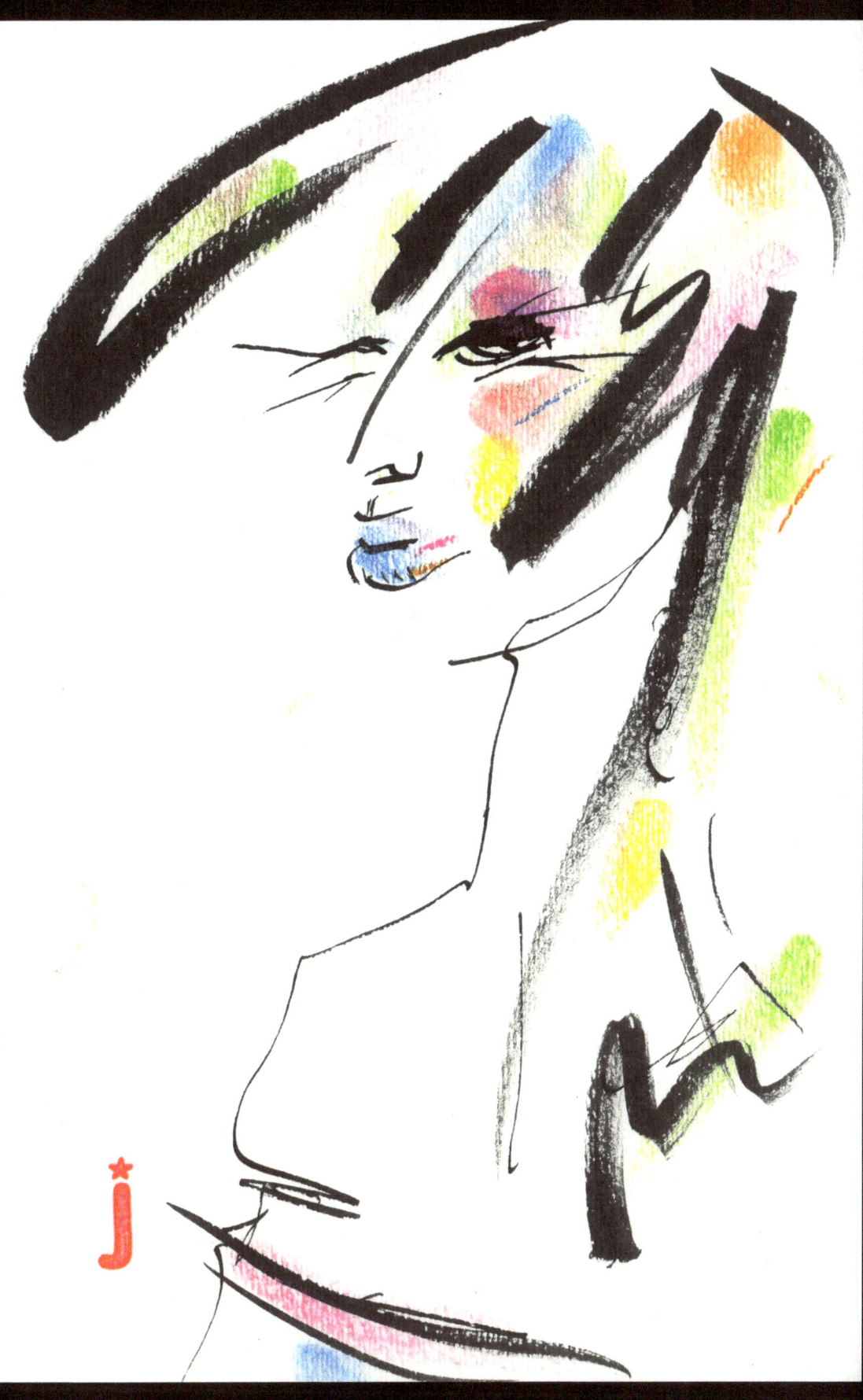

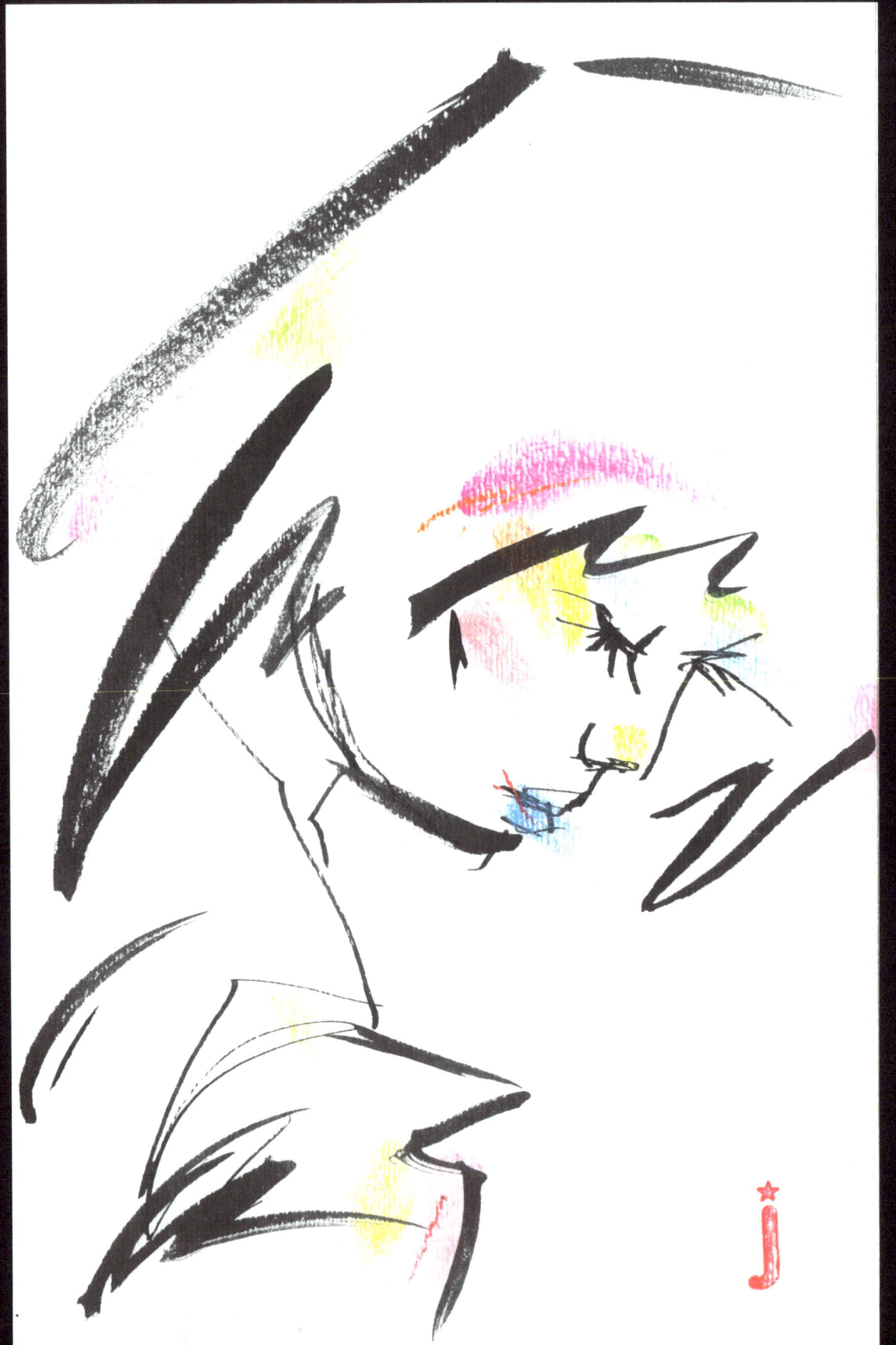

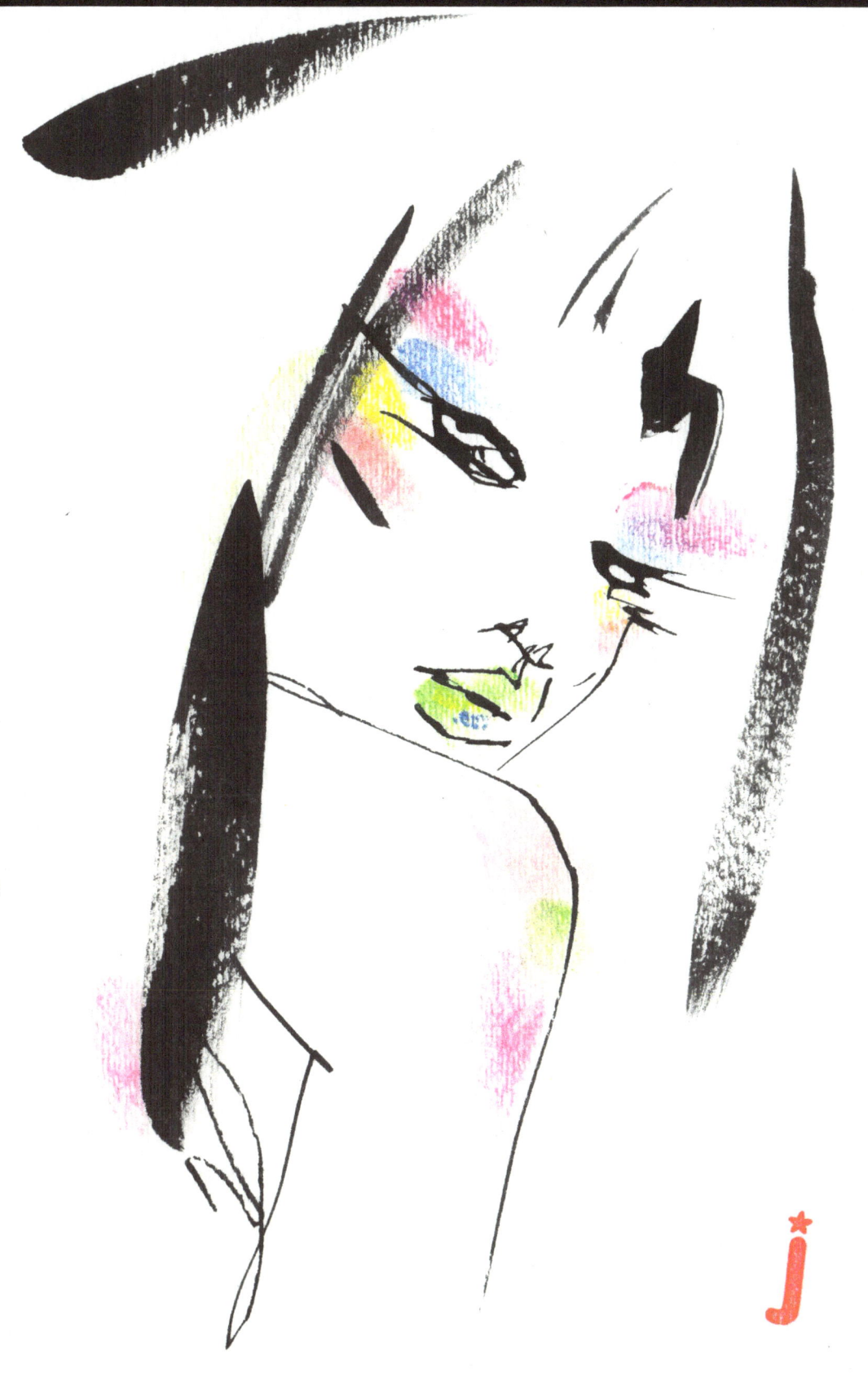

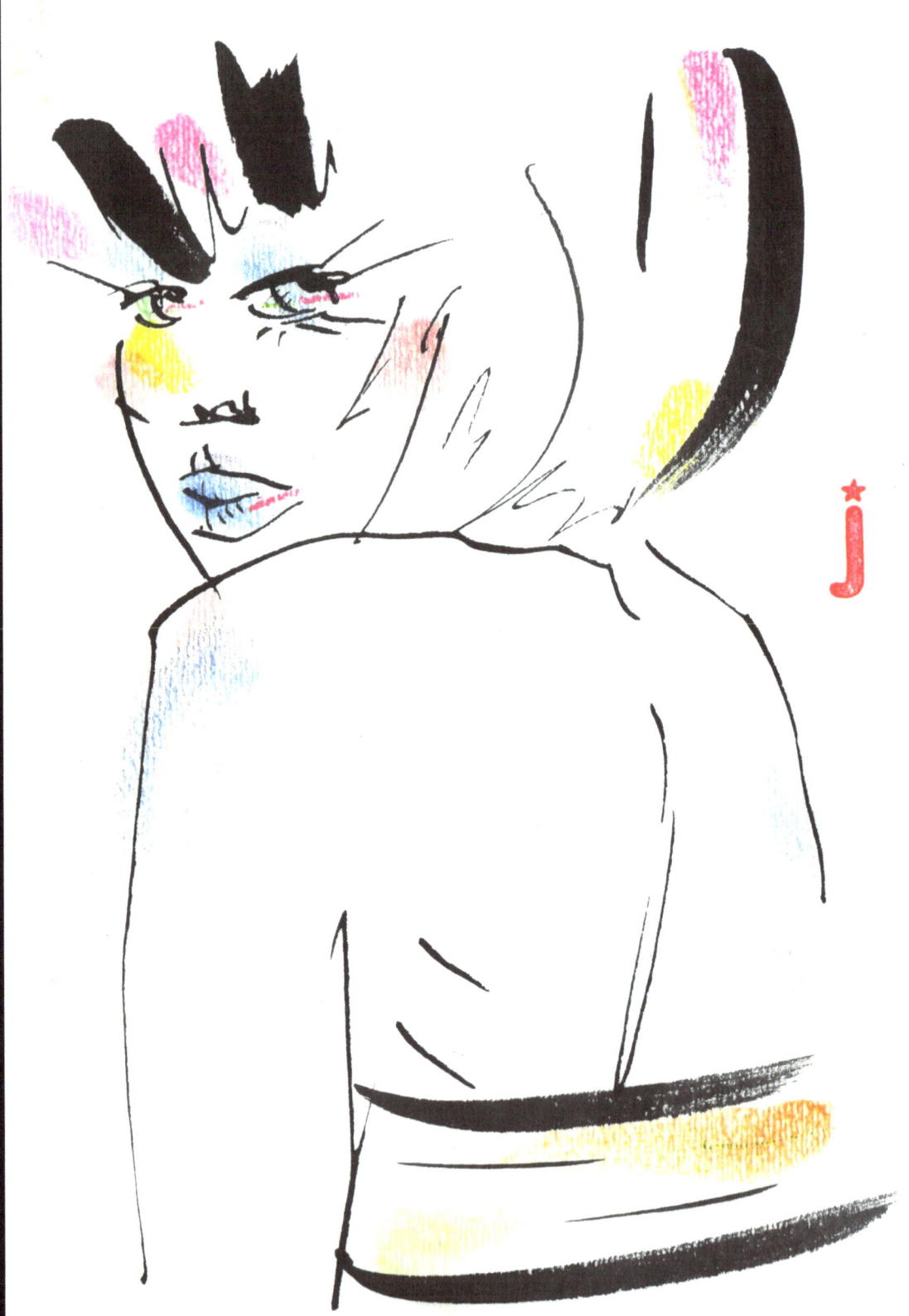

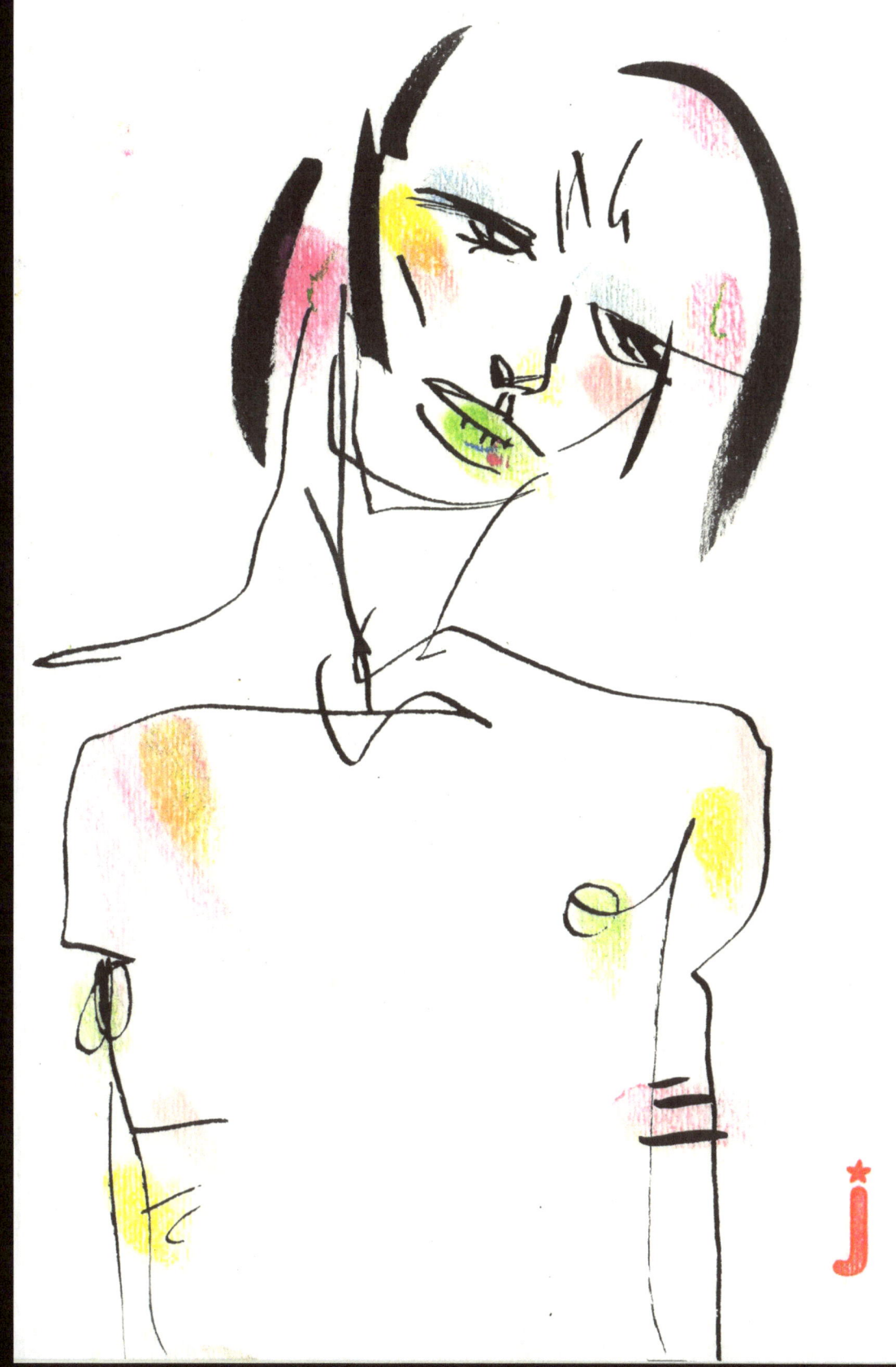

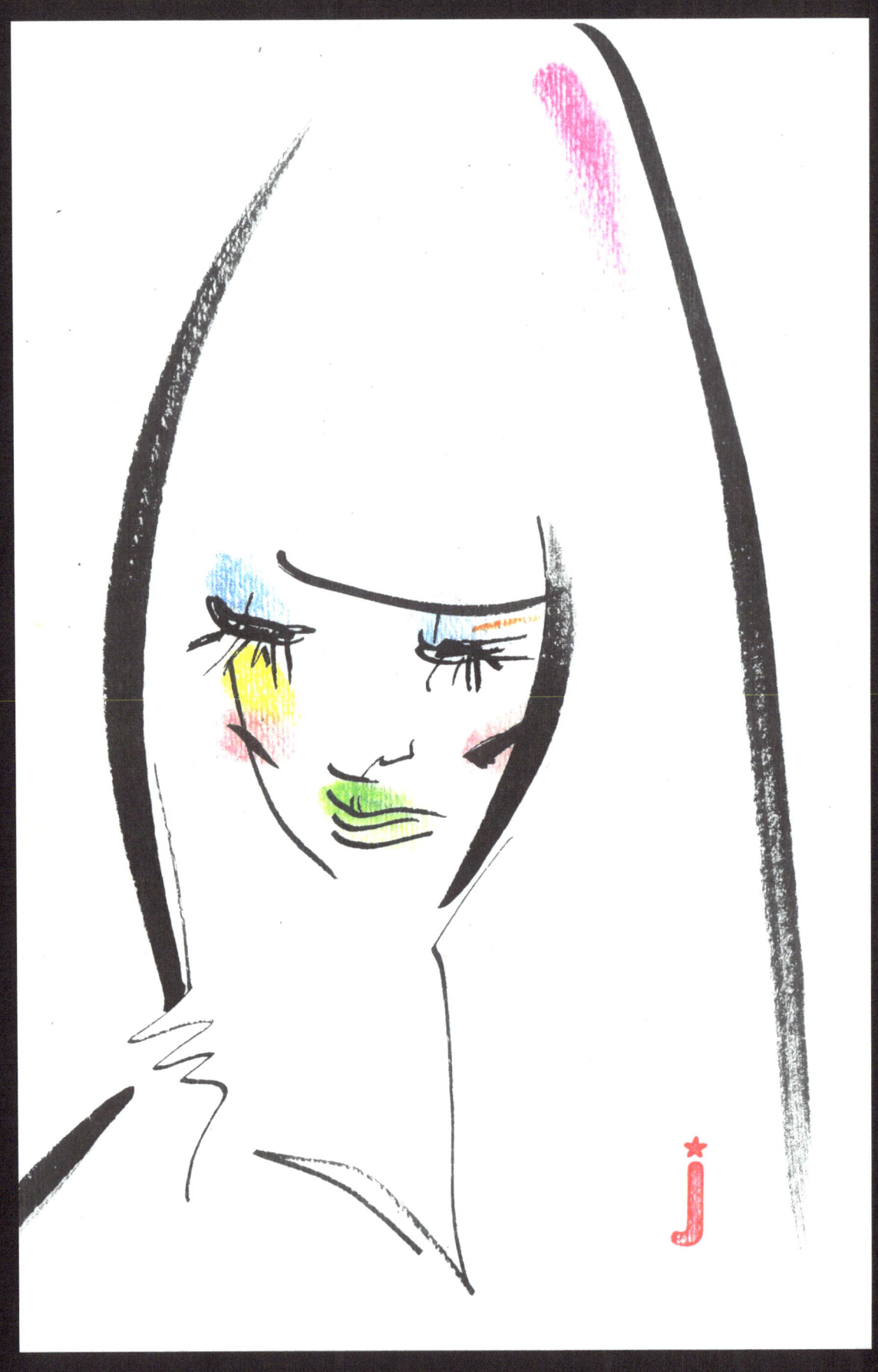

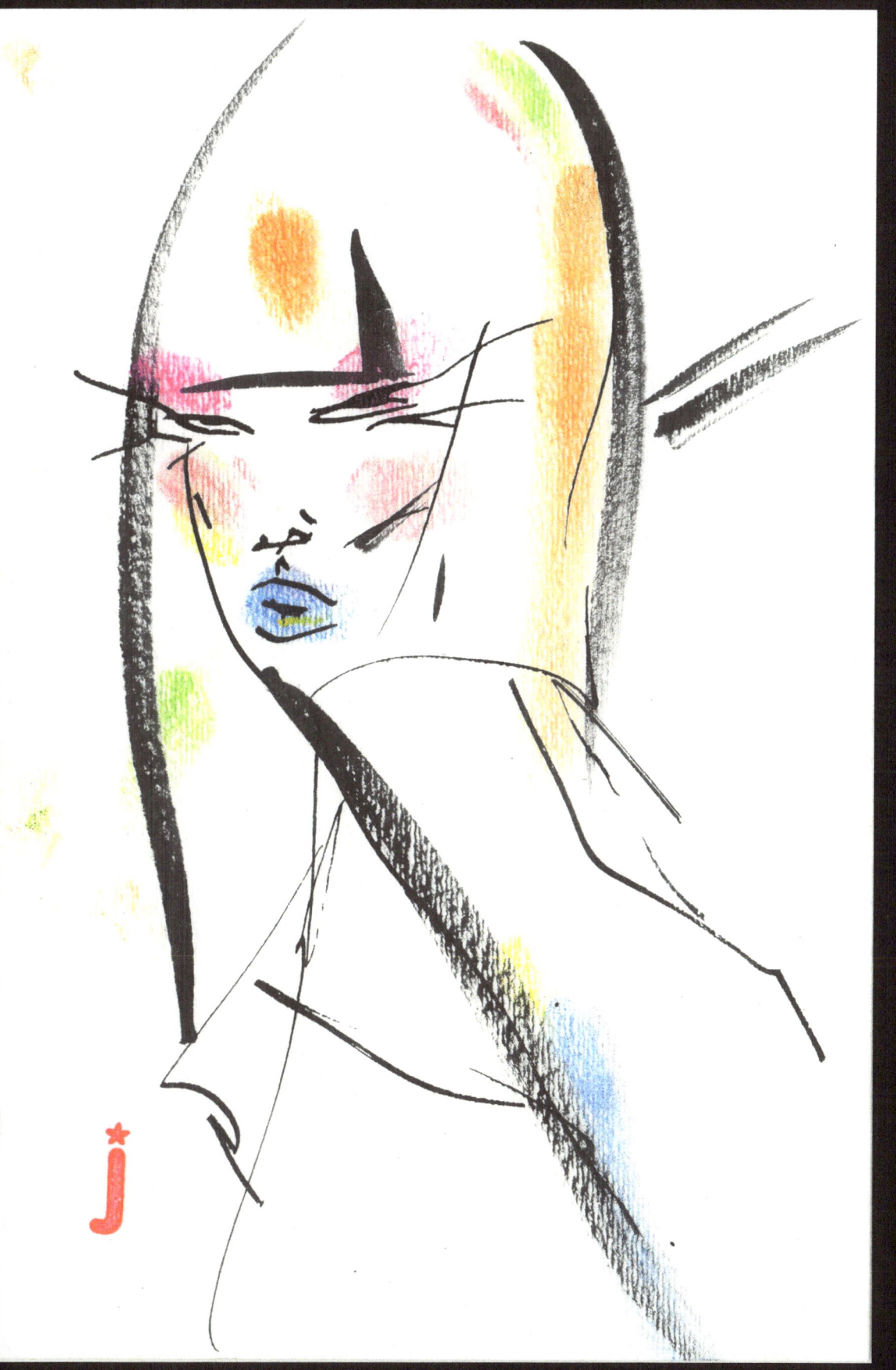

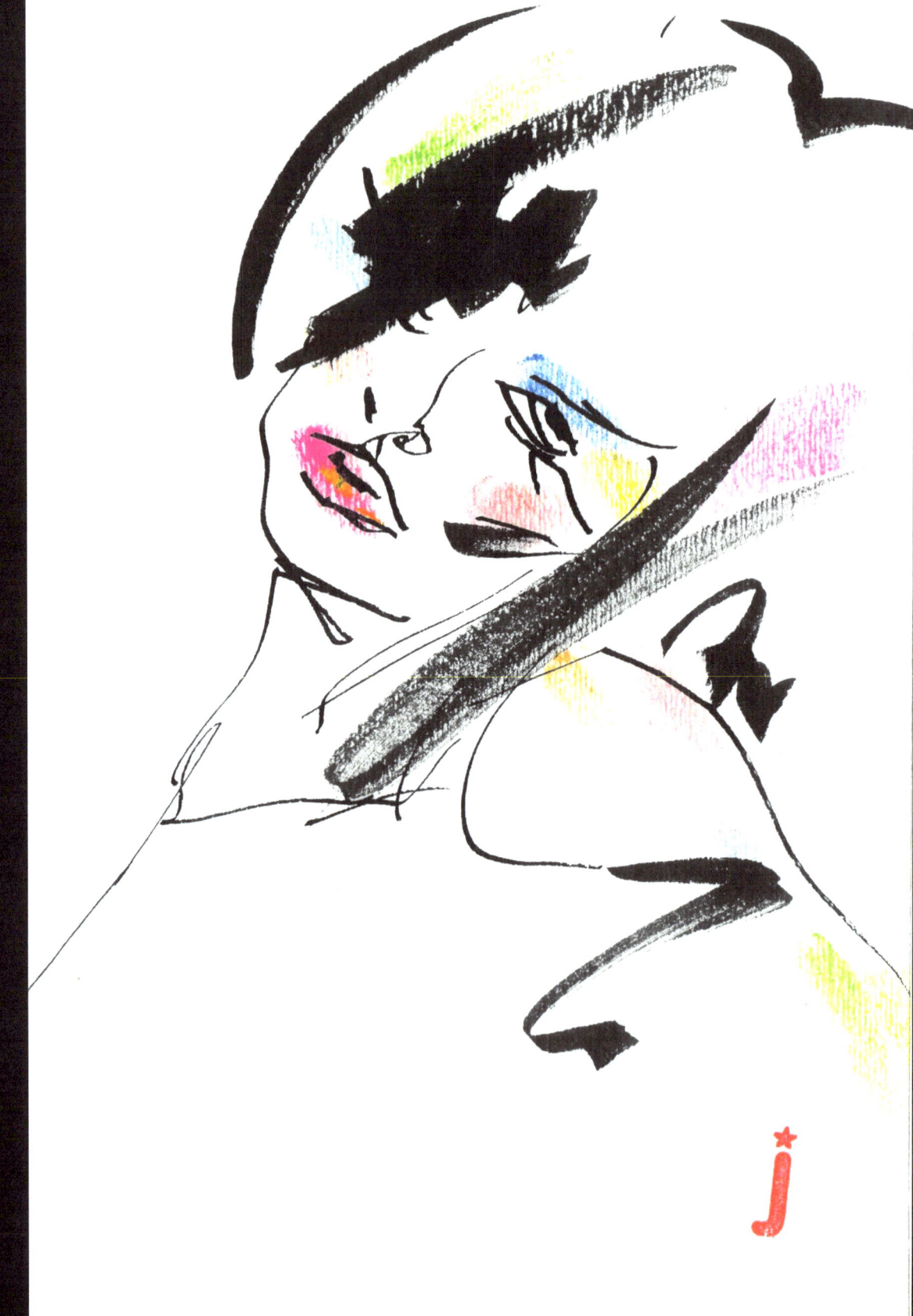

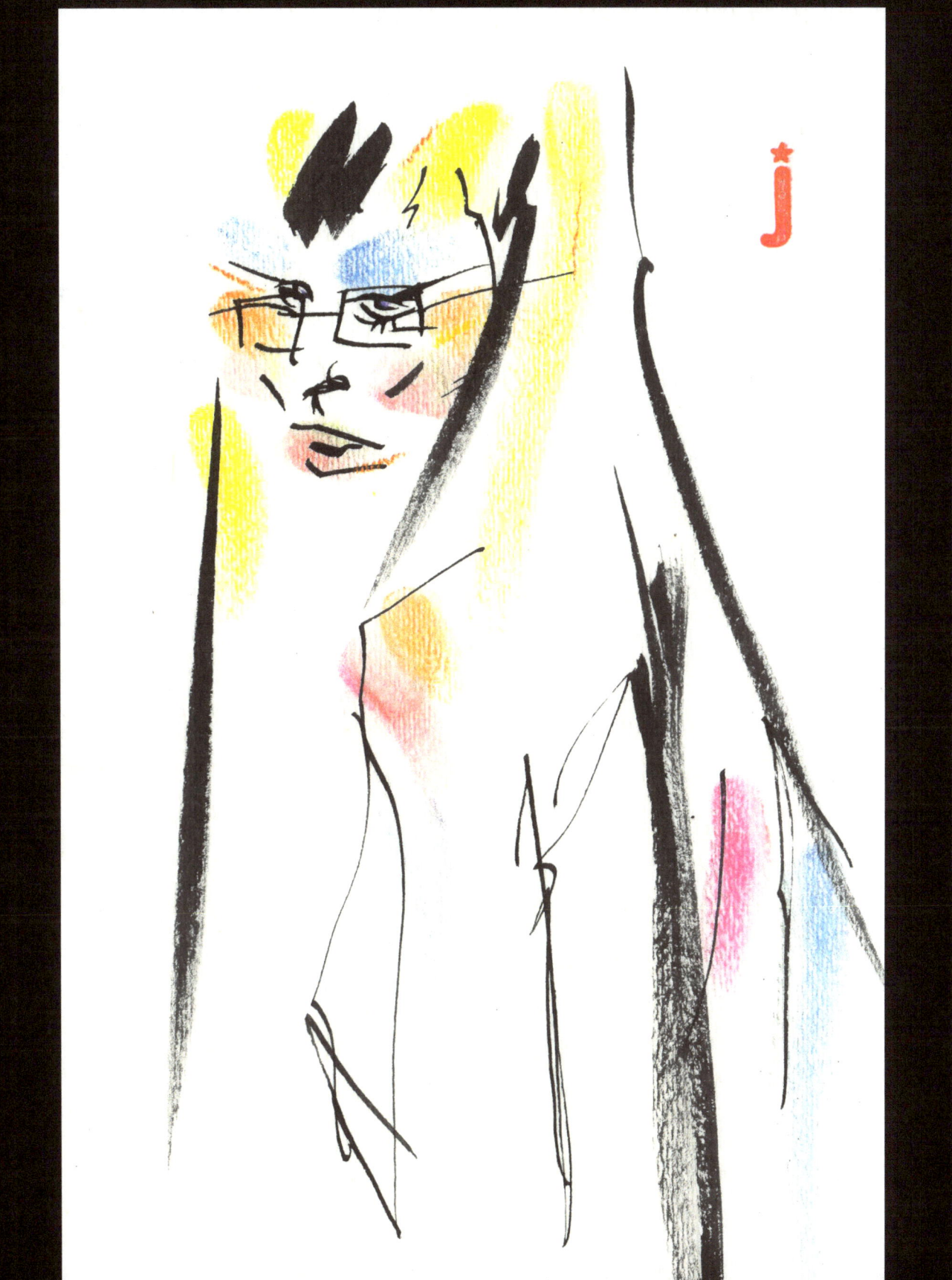

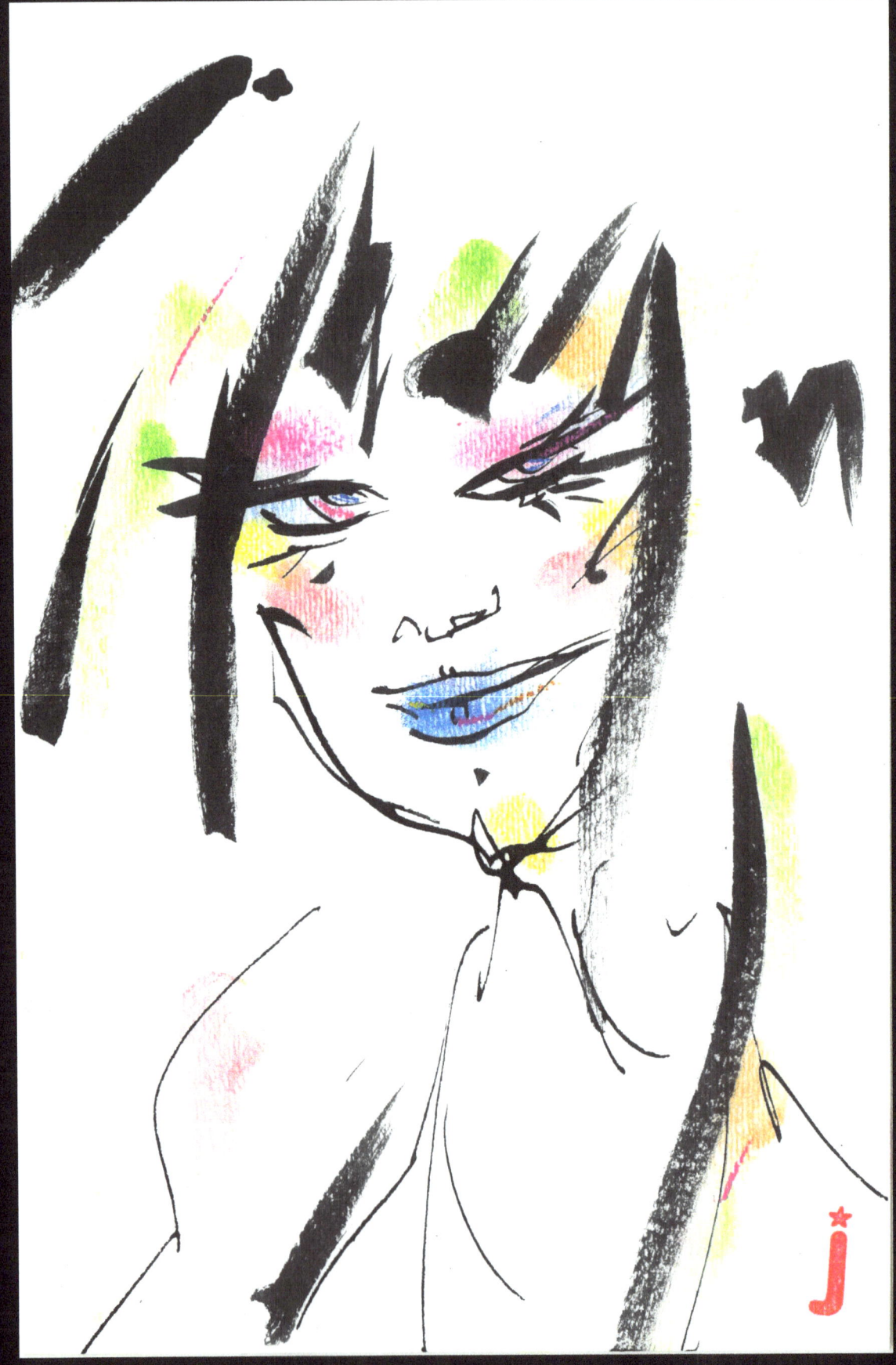

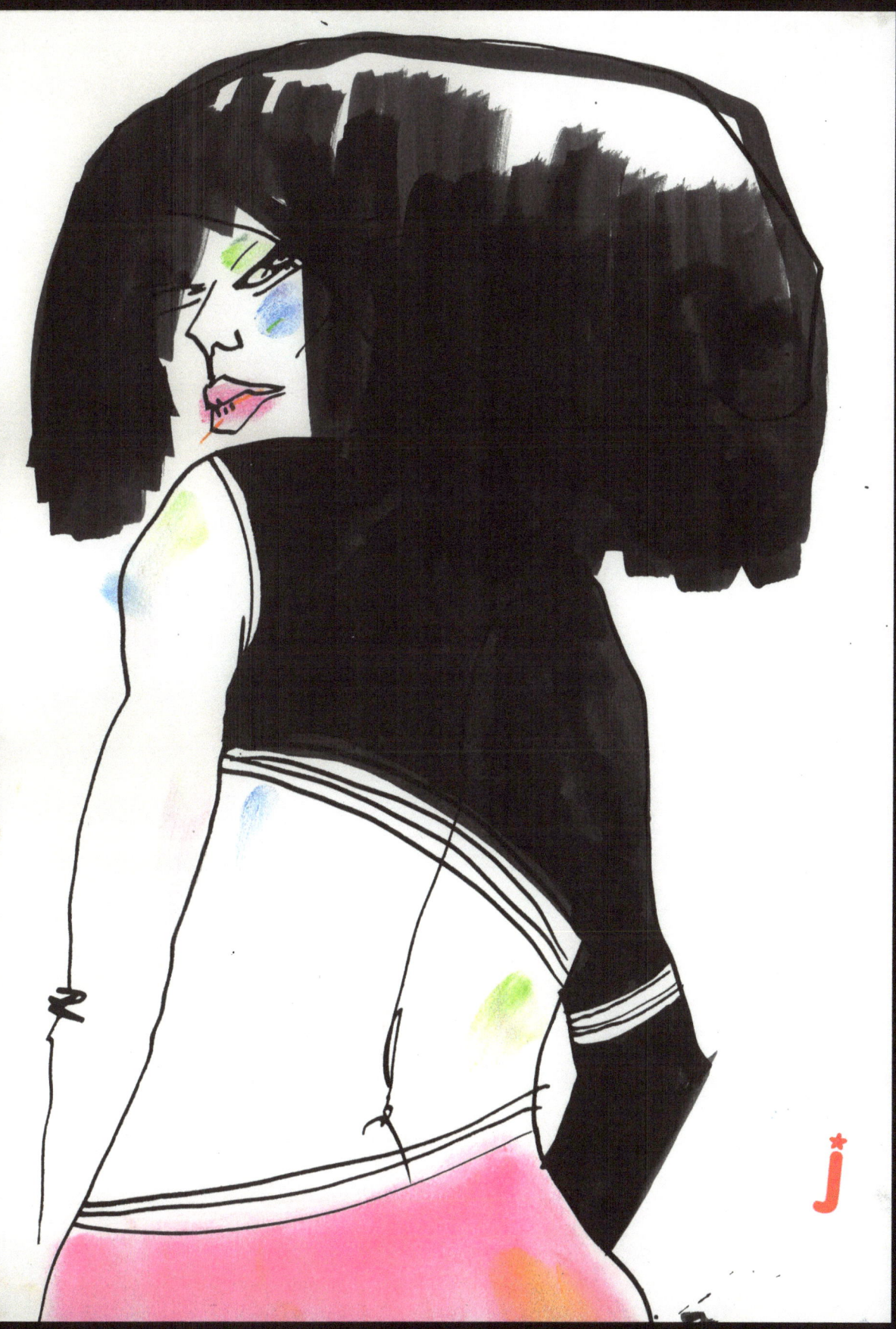

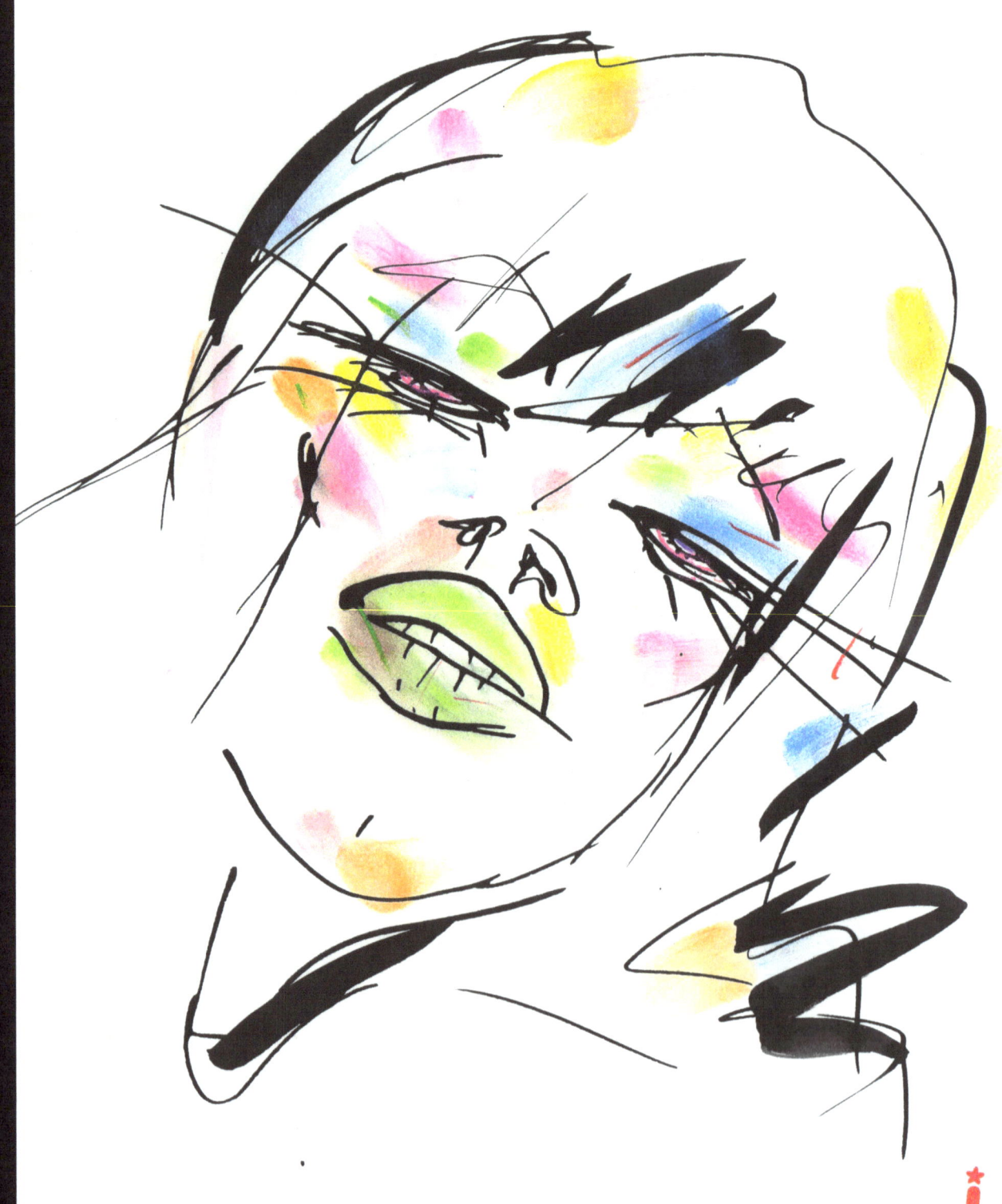

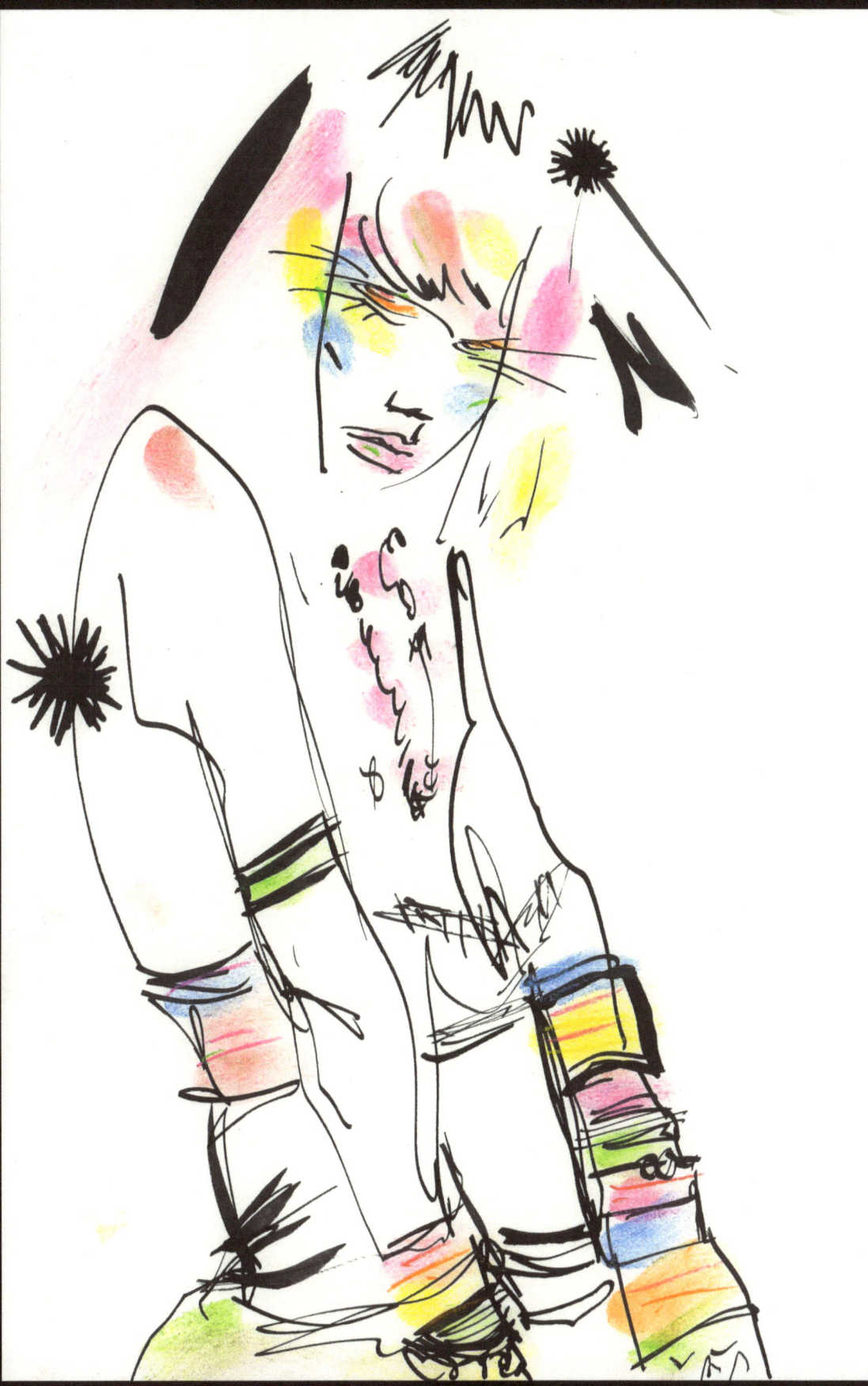

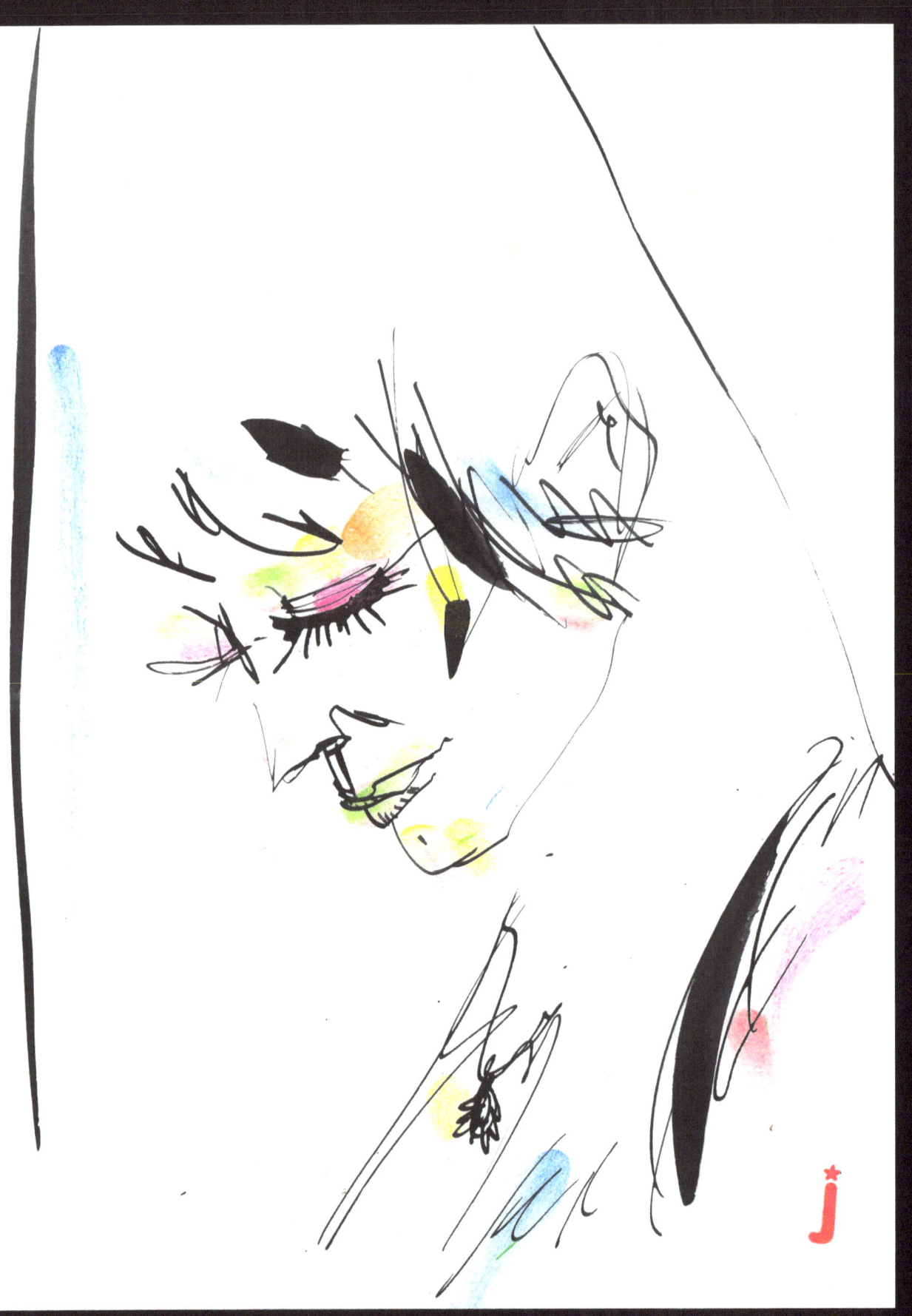

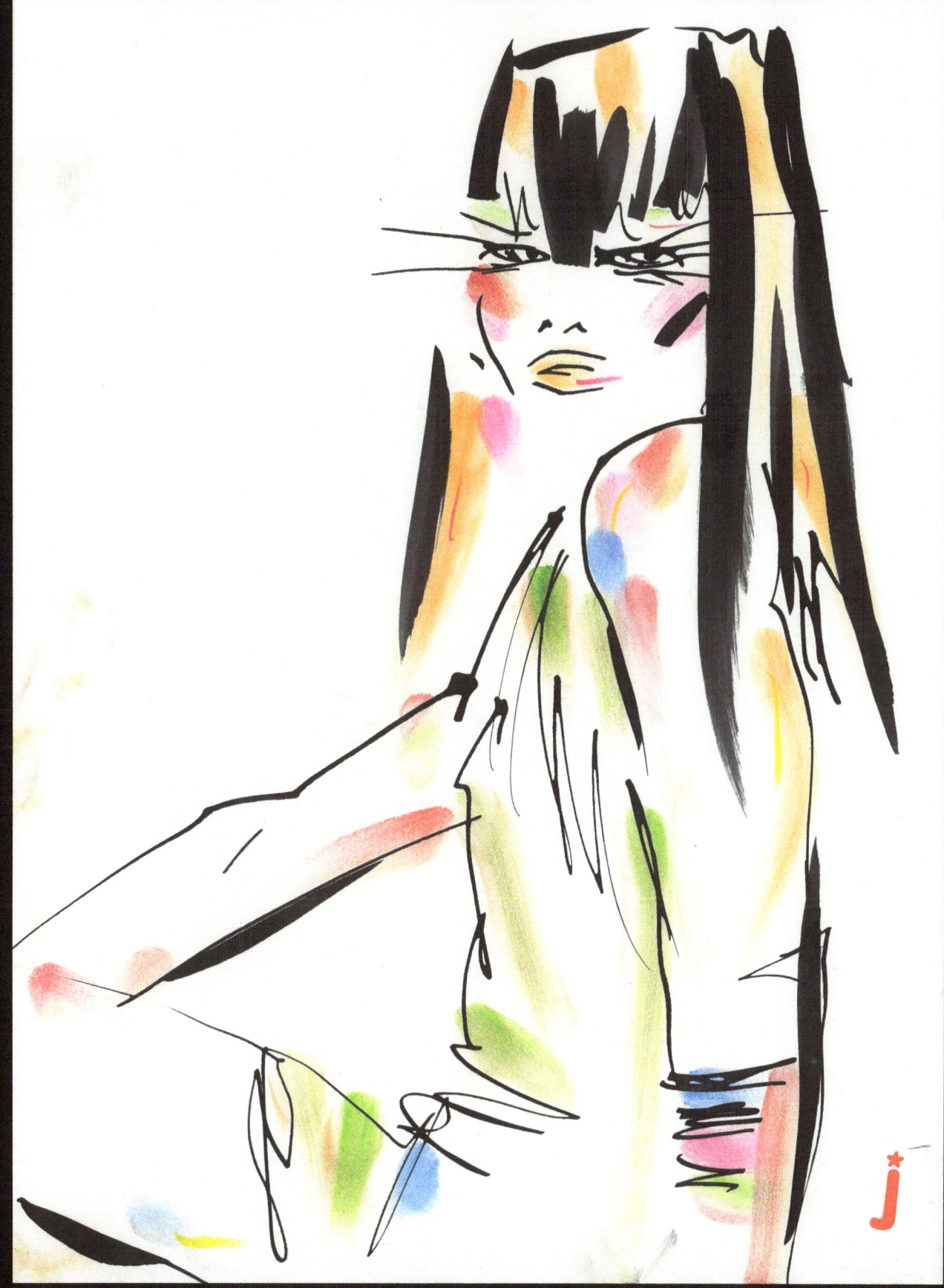

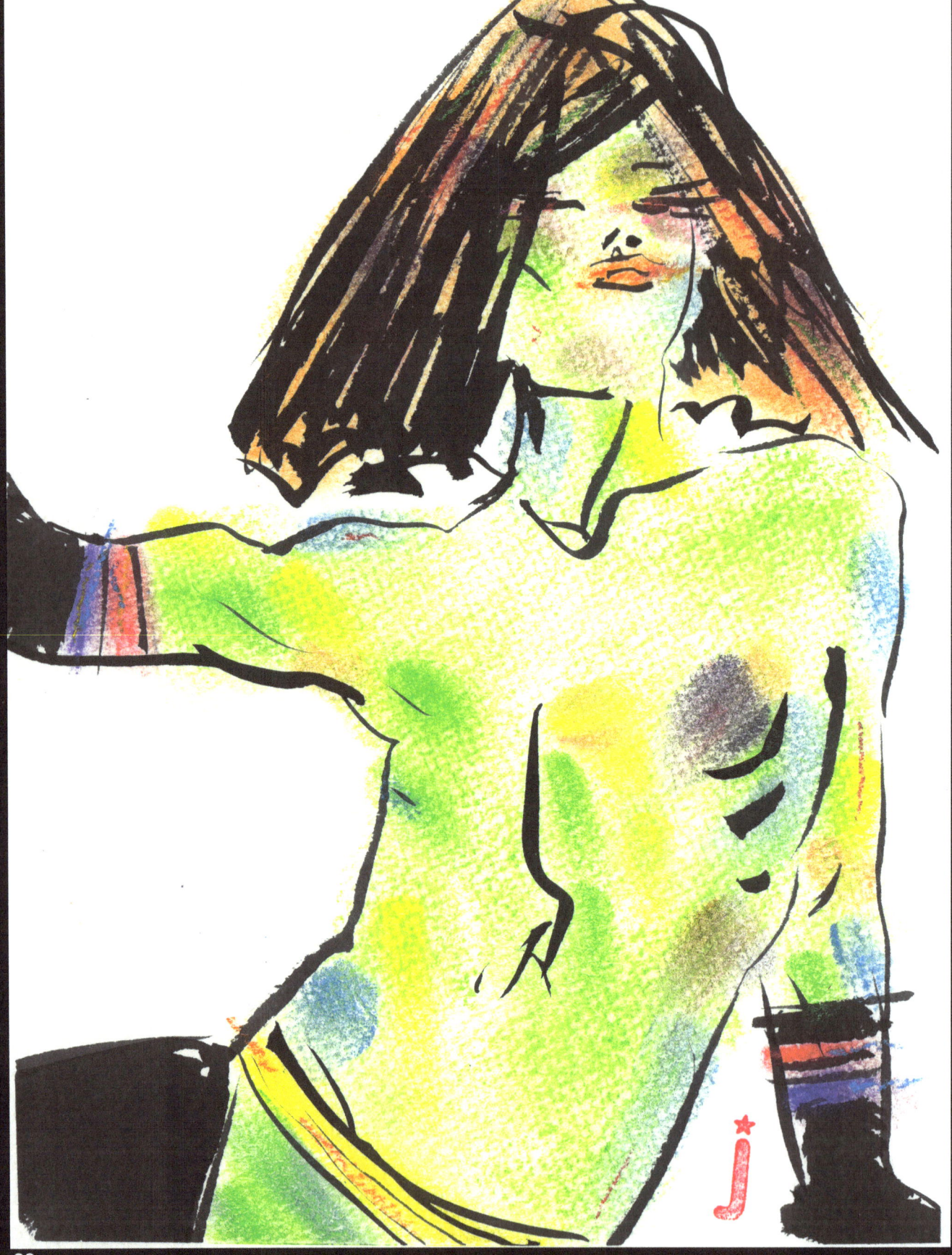

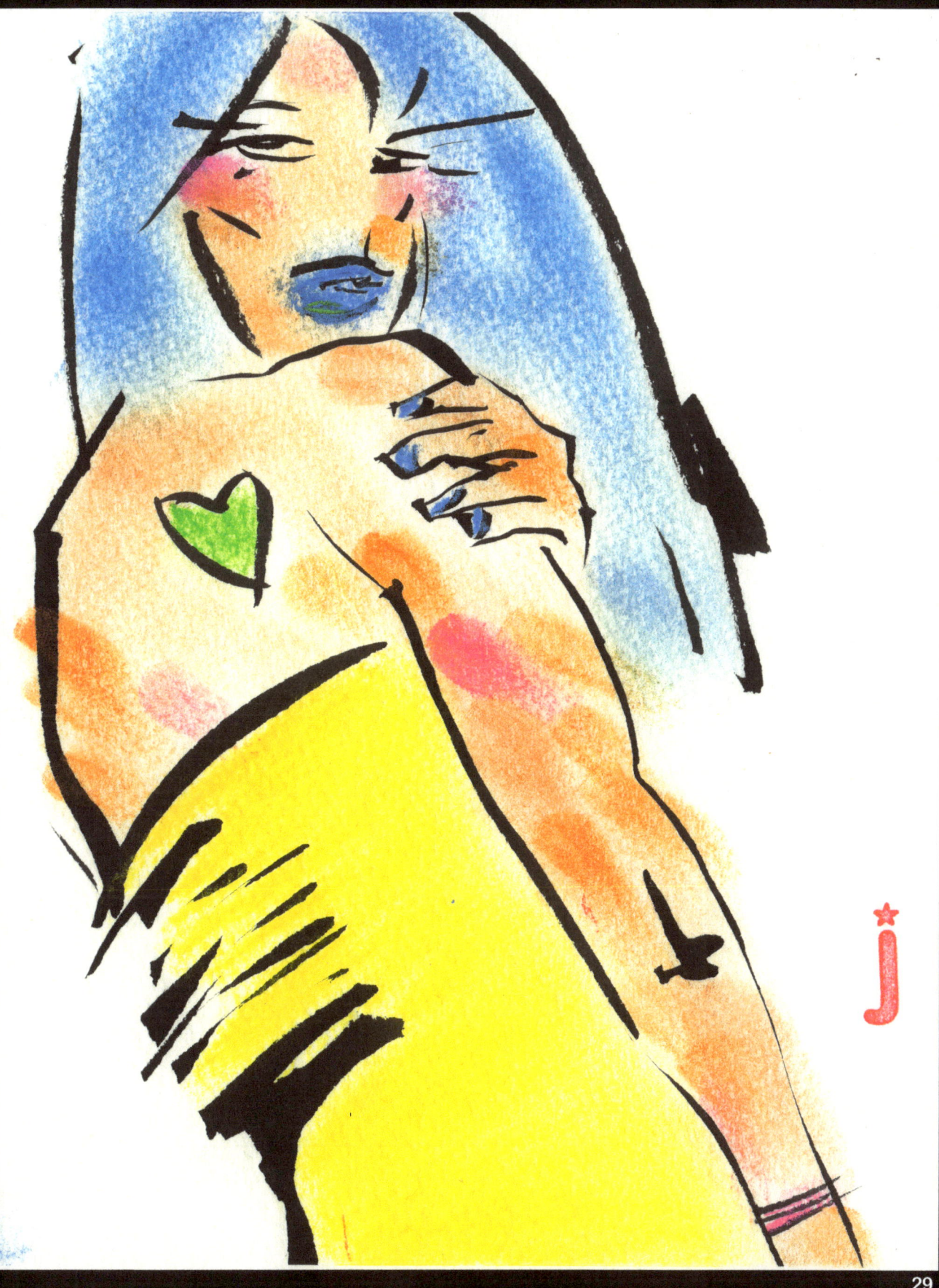

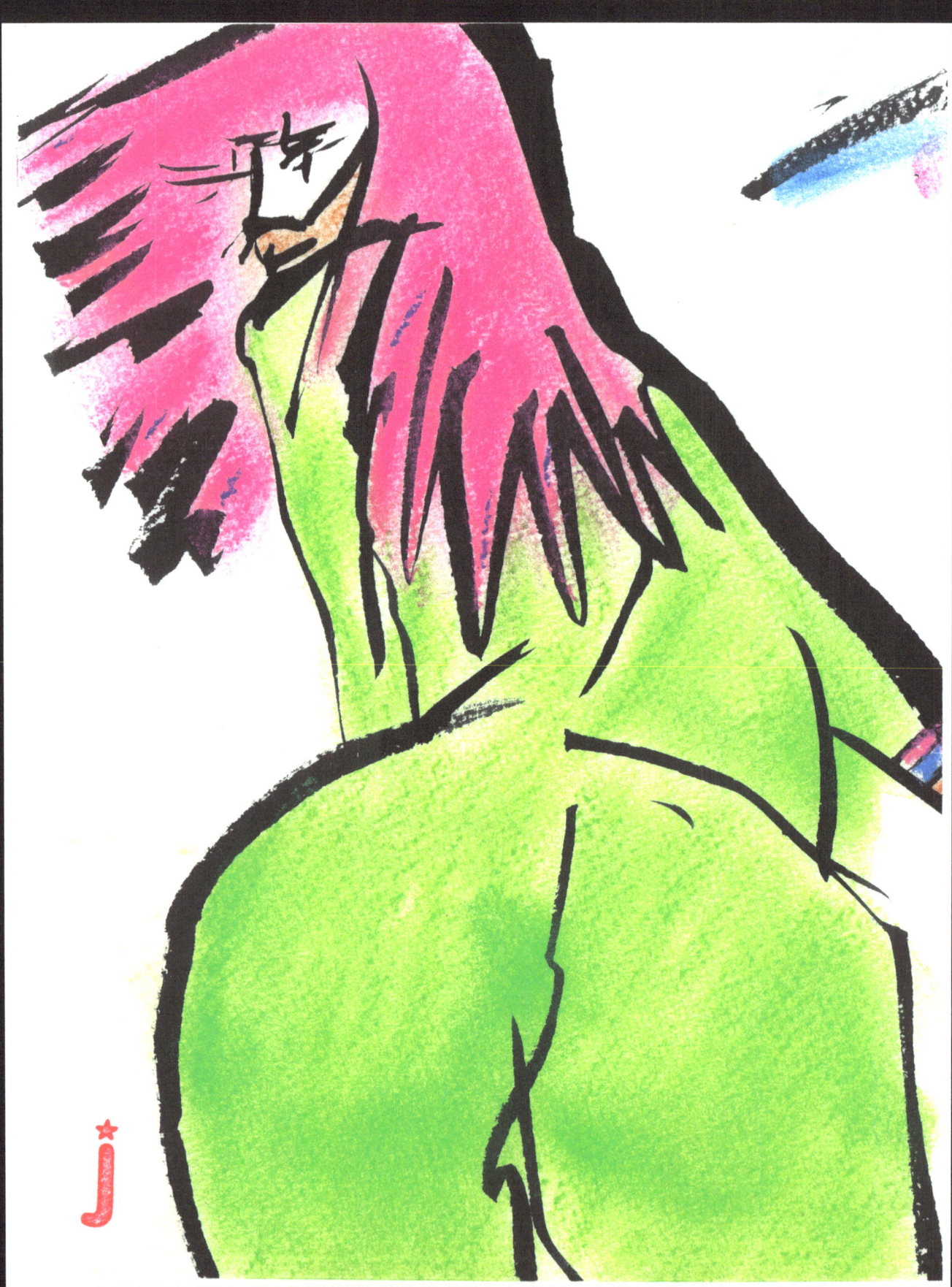

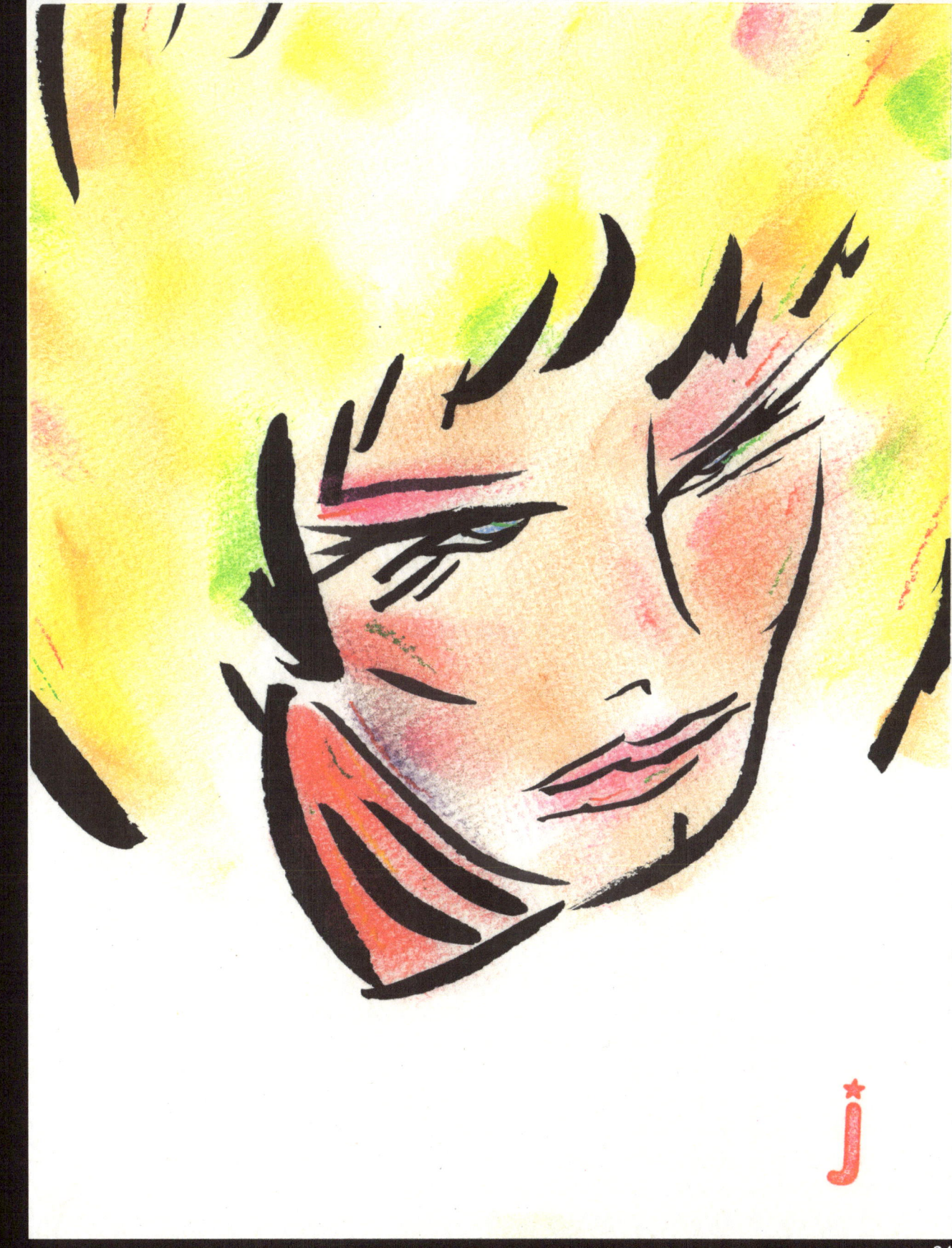

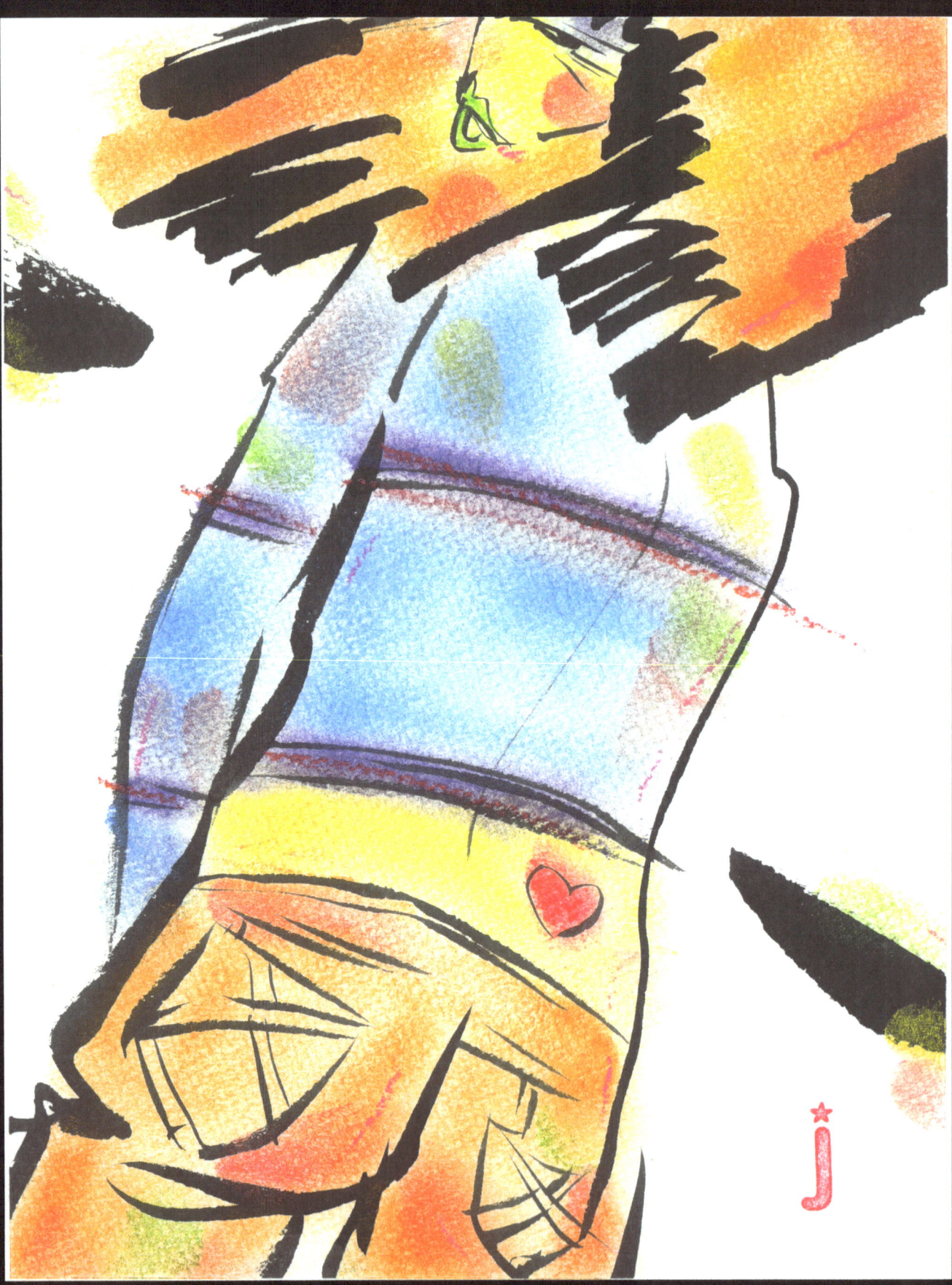

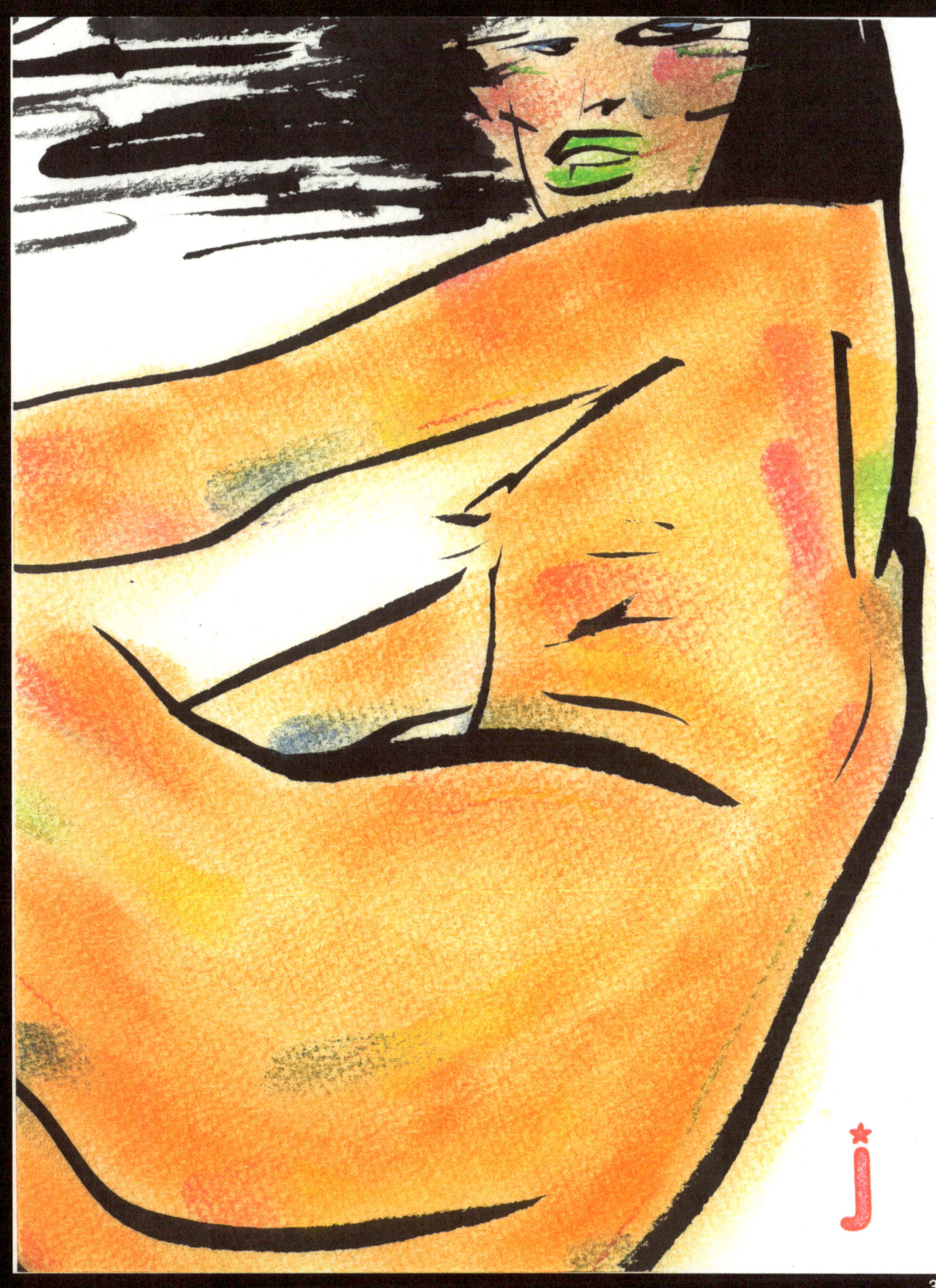

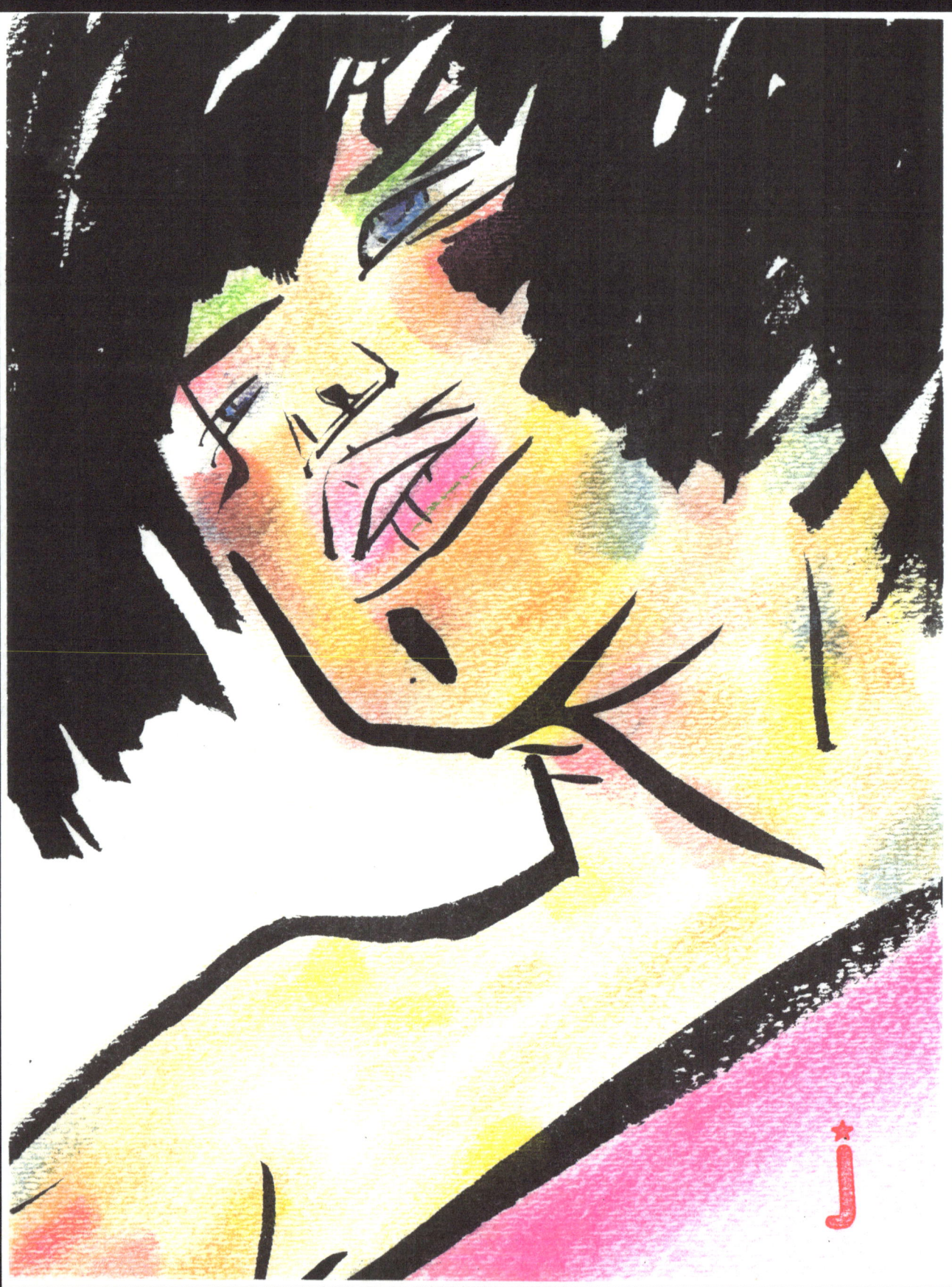

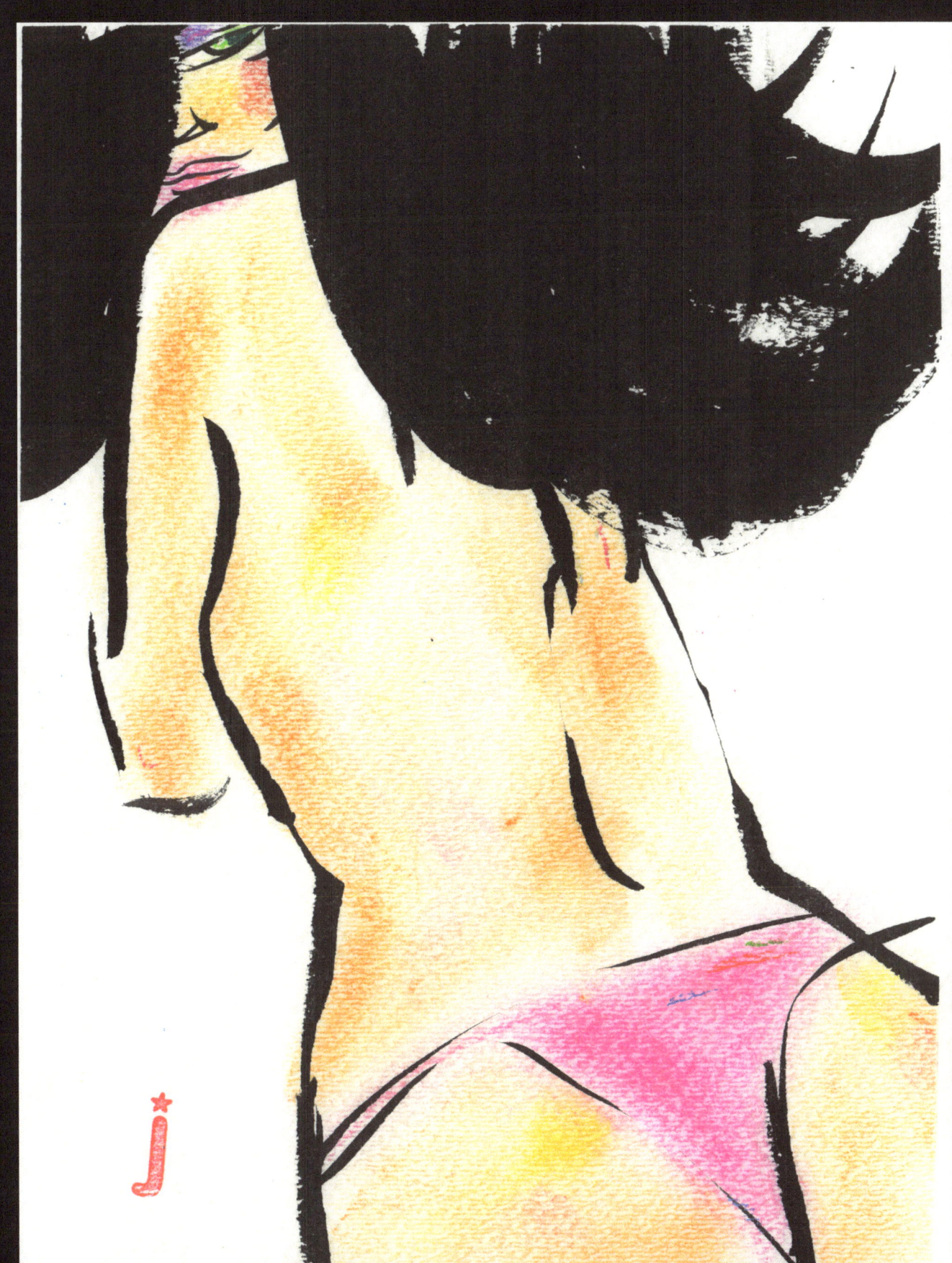

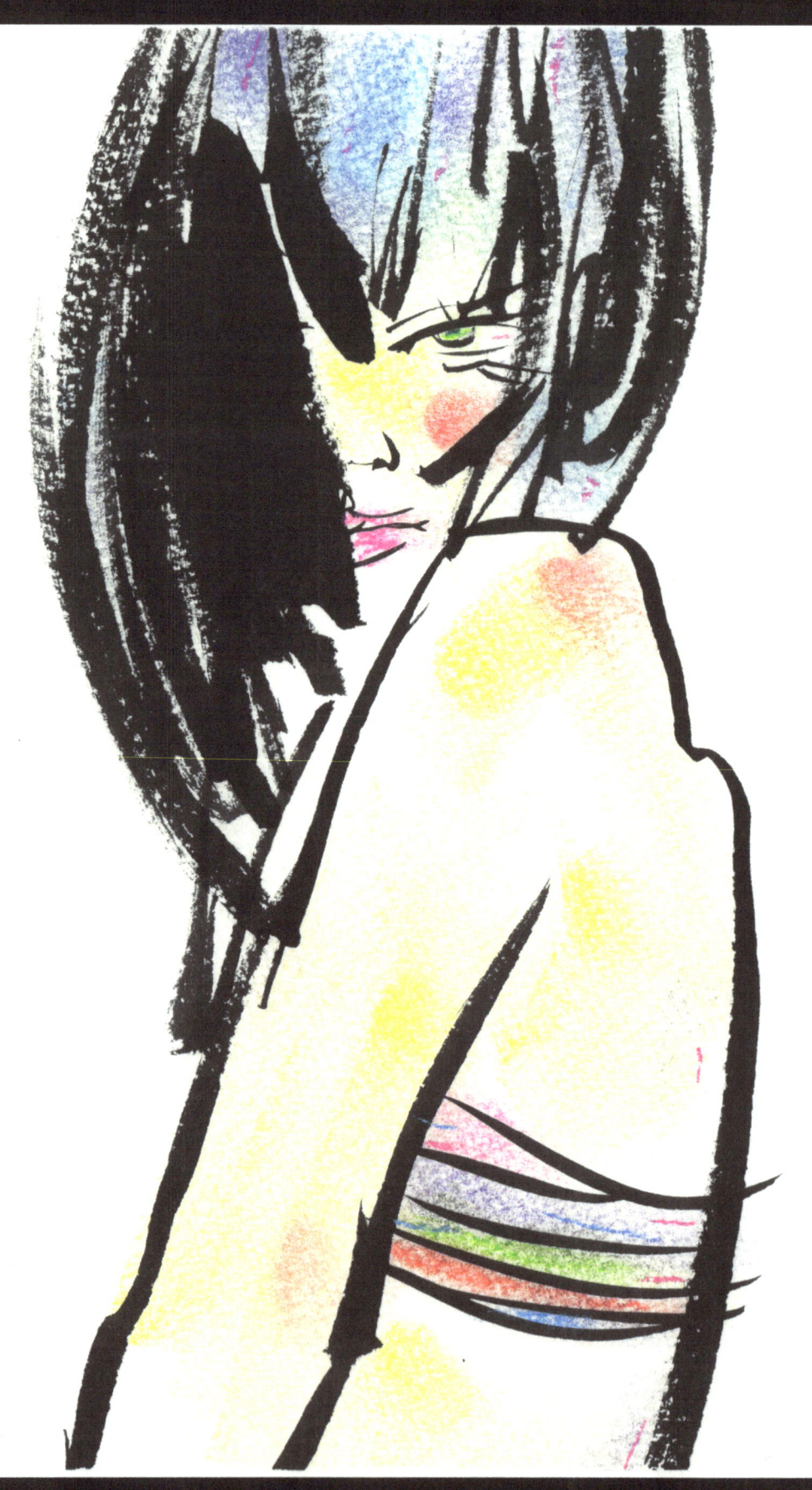

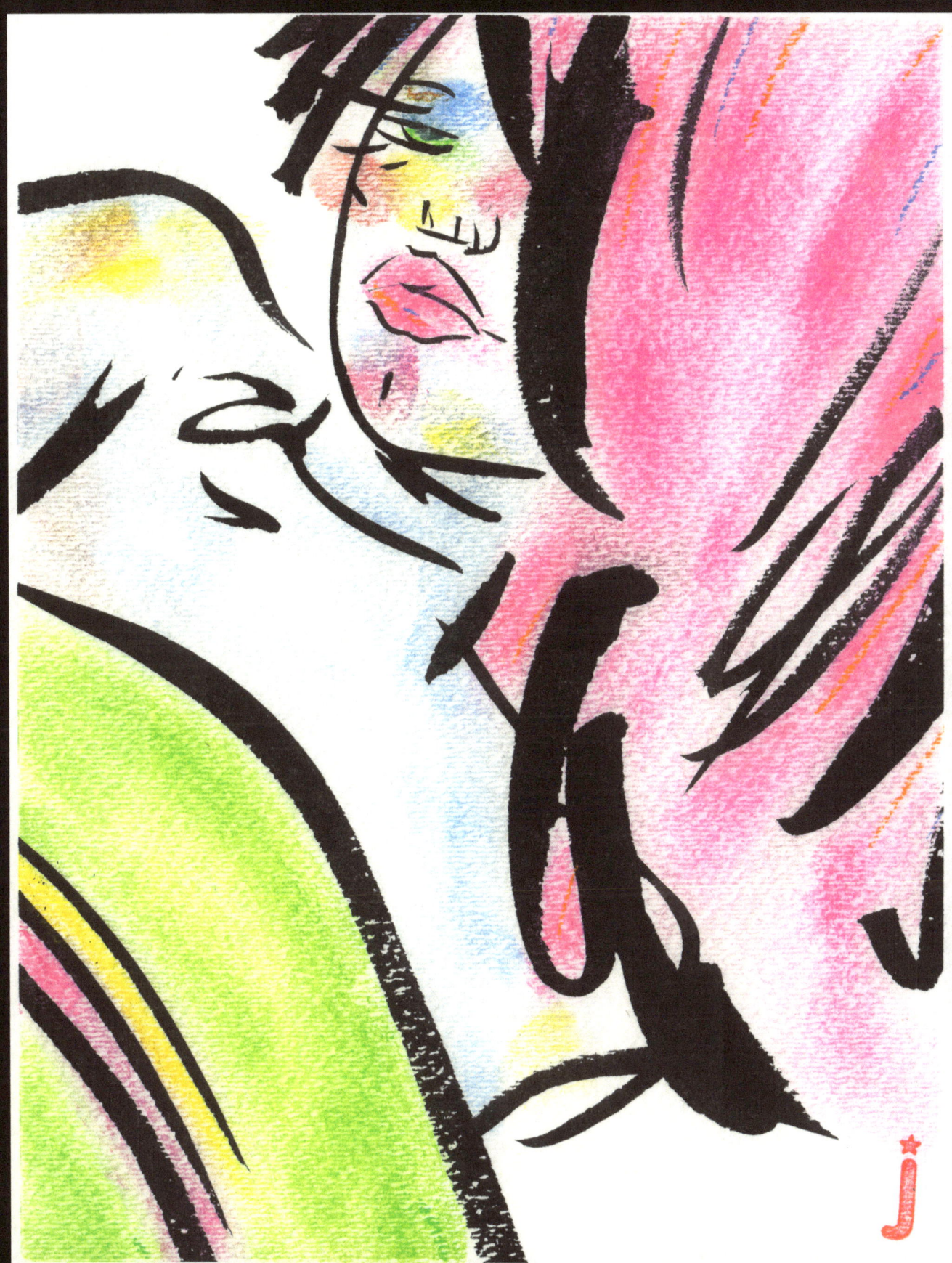

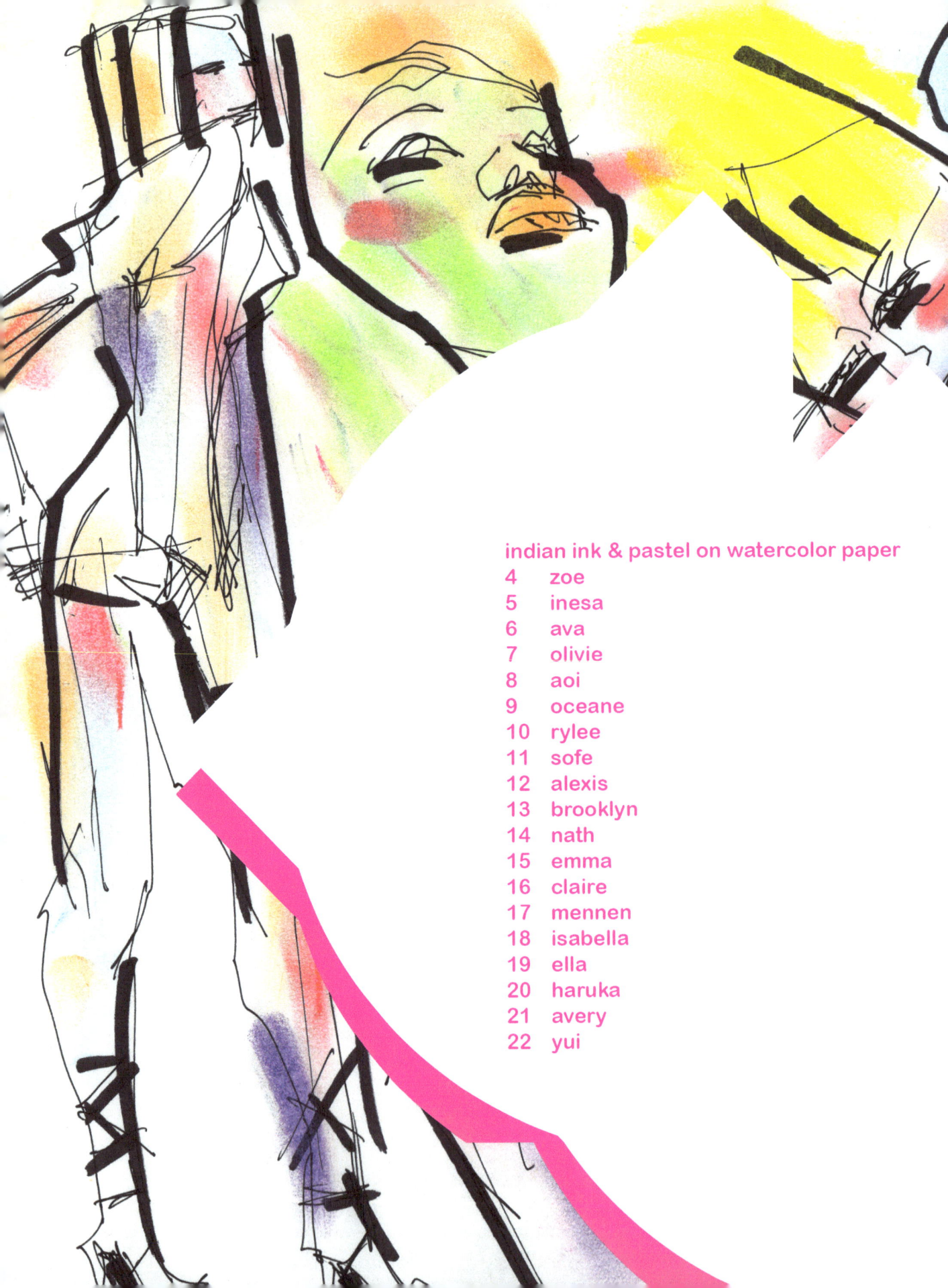

indian ink & pastel on watercolor paper

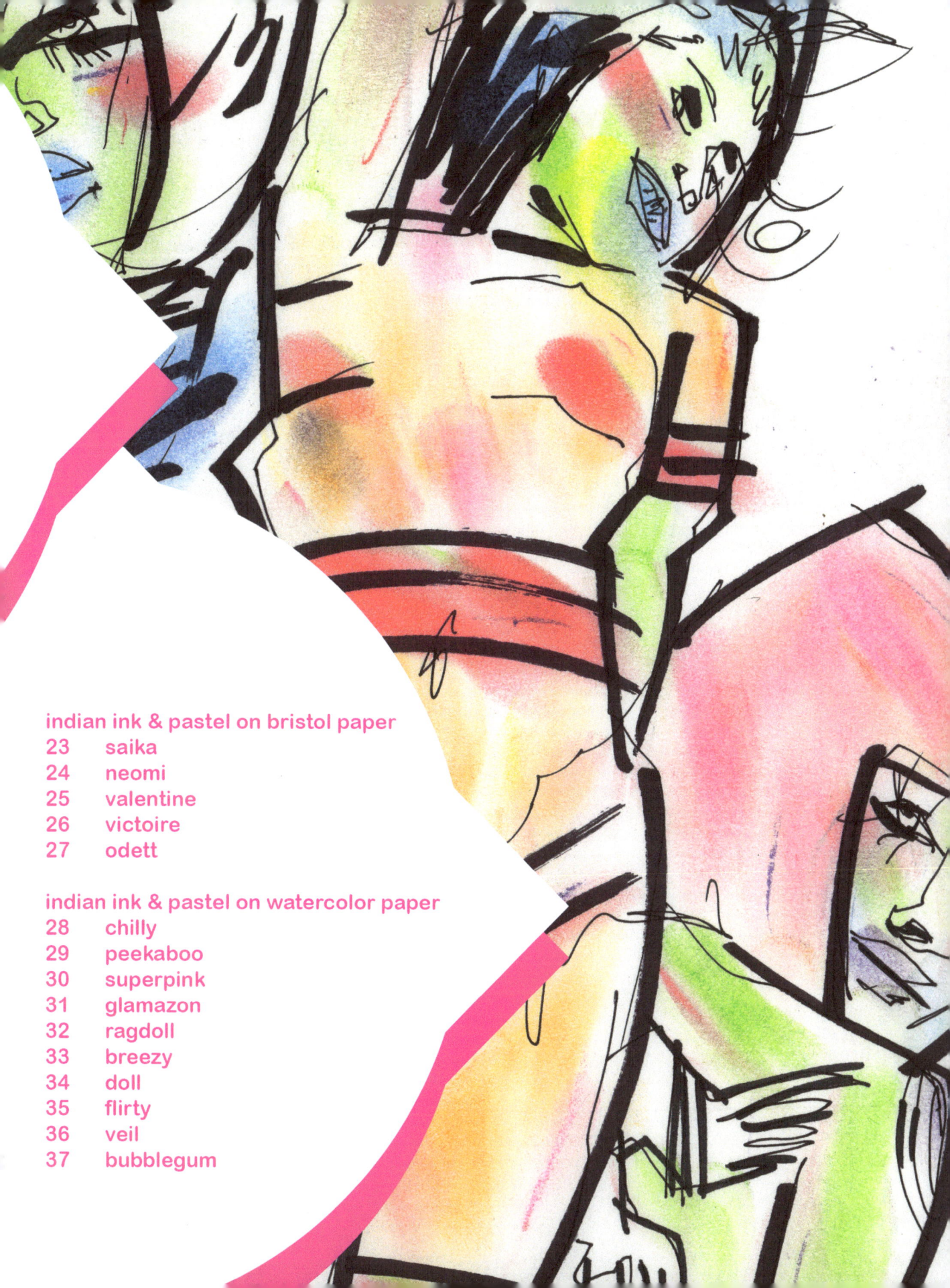

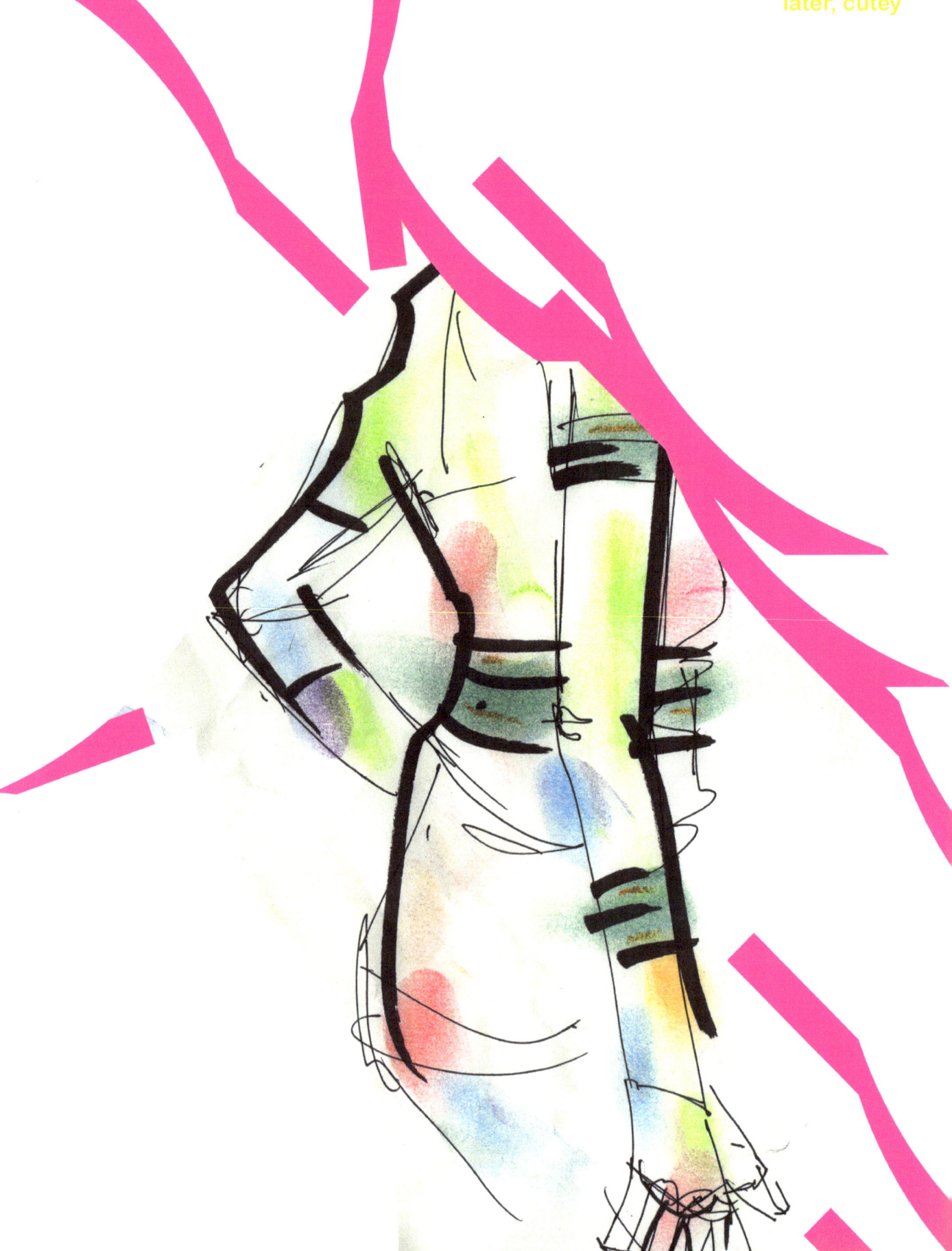